WOMEN IN THE OLYMPICS

WOMEN IN THE OLYMPICS

LINDSAY PARKS PIEPER AND JÖRG KRIEGER

First published in 2023
as part of the Sport and Society Book Imprint
doi: 10.18848/978-1-957792-47-7/CGP (Full Book)

Common Ground Research Networks
2001 South First Street, Suite 202
University of Illinois Research Park
Champaign, IL
61820

Copyright © Lindsay Parks Pieper and Jörg Krieger, 2023

All rights reserved. Apart from fair dealing for the purposes of study, research, criticism or review as permitted under the applicable copyright legislation, no part of this book may be reproduced by any process without written permission from the publisher.

Library of Congress Cataloging-in-Publication Data

Names: Pieper, Lindsay Parks, 1985- editor. | Krieger, Jörg, editor.
Title: Women in the Olympics / Lindsay Pieper & Jörg Krieger.
Description: Champaign, Ill. : Common Ground Research Networks, 2023. |
  Series: Sport & society teaching pocketbook series ; vol 4 | Includes
  bibliographical references. | Summary: "Women in the Olympics traces the
  history of women in the Olympic Games. This pocket book offer details
  about important milestones in Olympic history and illustrates the
  salient themes that have shaped women's involvement in the Games. From
  ancient times to today, women have always had a tenuous position in the
  Olympics. Women eventually gained access to the Games; however, they
  remained beset by roadblocks. Certain sports remained off limits;
  Olympic officials introduced sex tests; the Olympics were inaccessible
  for women in certain countries; and women remained severely
  underrepresented in the Olympic governance structure. Women in the
  Olympics shows how women have continuously fought for increased
  opportunities as athletes, equal access to elite sports, and a place in
  the decision-making process"-- Provided by publisher.
Identifiers: LCCN 2022050778 (print) | LCCN 2022050779 (ebook) | ISBN
  9781957792460 (paperback) | ISBN 9781957792477 (pdf)
Subjects: LCSH: Women Olympic athletes--History. | Olympics--History. | Sex
  discrimination in sports--History.
Classification: LCC GV721.5 .W65 2023 (print) | LCC GV721.5 (ebook) | DDC
  796.48082--dc23/eng/20221026
LC record available at https://lccn.loc.gov/2022050778
LC ebook record available at https://lccn.loc.gov/2022050779

Cover photo: © LA84 Foundation

SPORT & SOCIETY POCKETBOOK TEACHING SERIES

The **Sport and Society Pocketbook Teaching Series** aims to introduce students and a general readership to relevant topics, theories, and concepts within sport history and sport sociology. The topics will vary but are united in their purpose to serve as an accessible alternative to generic textbook offerings or academic research monographs. We hope that the shorter and more accessible pocketbook format of the series will mean that each book can be read in an hour or two on a quiet evening or while commuting on a bus or train. This aligns with our ethos of accessibility in scholarly communication.

Books in the series can be accessed in print and electronic formats. In addition, and in parallel to both editions, each title will be accompanied by an online repository where additional learning and teaching resources are provided. The electronic platform for the series will include links to recent and significant research articles, visual materials, podcasts, lectures, and more, thus securing ongoing relevance by providing new and engaging resources and perspectives aligned with the topic of each book.

This series is for teachers, learners, and individuals with an interest in sports alike.

Dr. Jörg Krieger (Aarhus University, Denmark)
Dr. April Henning (University of Stirling, United Kingdom)
Dr. Lindsay Parks Pieper (University of Lynchburg, United States)
Dr. Jesper Andreasson (Linnaeus University, Sweden)

TABLE OF CONTENTS

Introduction	*1*
Obstacles to Women's Participation in Sport	7
Fights for Inclusion	33
Women in the Cold War Olympics	61
The Limited Liberation of Women in the Olympics by the End of the Century	93
Conclusion – Olympic Strides and Hurdles	121
Notes	*131*
Appendix 1 – Women's Olympic Participation 1896-2022	*141*
Appendix 2 – Women's Disciplines/Sports Added, 1900-2022	*145*
Appendix 3 – Women's Debut by Country 1900-2016	*155*

ACKNOWLEDGEMENTS

We would like to thank Florence Carpentier and Ana Maria de Freitas Miragaya for their valuable comments that greatly improved this manuscript. This project was partly funded by the Aarhus Universitets Forskningsfond and a grant from the Dansk Kulturministeriets Forskningsudvalg.

INTRODUCTION

French Baron Pierre de Coubertin developed the modern Olympics as a way for men to develop character and display manliness. In the context of the international tensions of the nineteenth century, Coubertin believed an international sporting forum would revitalize the male population and encourage brotherly fraternity around the world. He suggested such a competition would "give the youth of all the world a chance of a happy and brotherly encounter which will gradually efface the peoples' ignorance . . . which feeds hatred, accumulates misunderstandings, and hurtles events along a barbarous path toward a merciless conflict."[1]

Women did not fit in Coubertin's early vision of his Olympic project. He believed the Olympics "must be reserved for men." According to the founder, women's sport was "impractical, uninteresting, ungainly, and . . . improper." Coubertin added that, "women have but one task, that of crowning the winner with garlands."[2] Women therefore did not make an appearance at the first modern Olympics in 1896 as Coubertin invited only male athletes in selected male sports. Despite Coubertin's resistance, women slowly joined the Olympic Movement. Twenty-two female Olympians participated in croquet, equestrianism dressage, golf, sailing, and tennis at the 1900 Paris Games; their participation was later officially acknowledged by the International Olympic Committee (IOC), the non-governmental sport organization responsible for the Olympic Movement. When the Olympics returned to Paris in 1924, 135 women competed in diving, fencing, swimming, and tennis. Women have been fighting to achieve gender equality in Olympic participation ever since.

Coubertin may not have been able to bar women entirely from the early Olympics, but he did help limit the activities in which they competed. IOC members and International Federation (IF) leaders more willingly permitted women's participation in events that required grace and flexibility, such as diving and tennis, than those that required muscles and strength, such as athletics and basketball. Sports considered too physical or grueling remained off limits to women for most of the twentieth century. For example, the IOC barred women from track and field, the most popular and important Olympic sport at the beginning of the century, until 1928 (see chapter two). Team sports remained reserved for men until 1964, when women played volleyball for the first time (see chapter three). Olympic organizers featured the men's marathon in every Olympics since 1896; women did not participate until 1984 (see chapter four). Only men competed in the 3,000m steeplechase until 2008, boxing until 2012, ski jumping until 2014, and sprint and slalom canoeing until 2020. As of 2022, women have not yet competed in the 50km race walk, decathlon, Nordic combined, or Greco-Roman wrestling at the Olympics.[3]

In addition to limiting women's opportunities as athletes, Coubertin also formed the IOC, in 1894, entirely of men. The IOC enforces the rules of the Olympic Charter and oversees the organization of the Olympic Games. His first four presidential successors similarly only appointed men to serve. As historians Kay Schiller and Christopher Young explain, throughout most of its existence, the IOC "behaved on occasion with the random unaccountability of a self-electing gentleman's club."[4] It was an all-male group for over eighty years until Pirjo Häggman of Finland and Flor Isava Fonseca of Venezuela joined as members in 1981. Their entrance occurred under the leadership of Juan Antonio Samaranch, the IOC's sixth president. From their participation as Olympians to their roles as decision makers, women spent much of their time in the Olympics on the sidelines.

In other words, women have had a shaky place in the Games for over one hundred years. Since the beginning of the Olympics, women have had to fight for inclusion as athletes and leaders. Their tenuous position in the Olympic Movement has far-reaching consequences. The Olympics are the most influential, international multi-sport event in the world. In conversation with local organizing committees, the IOC determines which sports and events are contended, and how. This, in turn, shapes participation trends around the globe. For example, when the IOC added baseball for men and softball for women at the 2020 Tokyo Olympics, it reinforced gendered perceptions of the two sports.[5] Even though women play baseball and men play softball, the IOC's decision reinforced the idea that they are activities separated by gender. Because of the importance of the Olympics—athletically, financially, and socially—women have fought for increased access since the beginning. This pocketbook traces the incremental progress they forged against constant waves of backlash.

Chapter one illustrates the male-dominated mindset and organization of the ancient and early modern Olympics. Modern sport developed in the mid-1800s as an avenue for boys and men to develop masculinity. Sport leaders therefore did not encourage women's participation in physical activities. Sharing this mentality, Coubertin limited women's participation in his Olympic Games. He discouraged their participation entirely at the 1896 Athens Olympics. However, the local Organizing Committees for the Olympic Games eventually allowed upper-class women to compete in certain events. Yet, they remained limited to separate, oftentimes modified competitions, participating only in those deemed acceptably feminine—activities practiced for aesthetic and health purposes with low physical efforts. Archery, golf, swimming, tennis, and yachting fell under this category.

Chapter two explores women's fight for inclusion. Limited to too few events in the male-controlled sporting forums, female leaders created their own, separate, international, multi-sport competitions. Led by French sport feminist Alice Milliat, the "Women's Olympics" sponsored women's participation in a range of sports throughout the 1920s and 1930s. This included track and field events, from which Olympic leaders excluded them entirely. Concerned about female leadership over women's sport, the IOC eventually relented in 1928 and included some track and field events for women. Yet, the male Olympic leaders embraced faulty science to limit the events in which women could compete. They also started to cast doubt on women who ran too fast or threw too far, introducing physical examinations for "suspicious" women to check their sex. These sex verification practices increased during the latter half of the twentieth century.

Chapter three sheds light on women during the Cold War Olympics. During this period, the sporting world split into East versus West. The Olympics gained new importance as Eastern and Western Bloc countries used the Games to demonstrate superiority without military confrontation. Women's sport grew as a result. However, with new opportunities came backlash. Female Olympians faced accusations of being male imposters and dopers, leading to the intensification of sex testing practices via the introduction of on-site, mandatory sex verification and doping controls.

Chapter four discusses women at the Olympics at the end of the twentieth century. Supported by the onset of the "second wave" women's liberation movement in some parts of the world, women gained new opportunities in the Olympics as athletes and leaders. Female Olympians demanded equal representation on the Olympic programme and in the Olympic boardroom. Progress was achieved in many ways; however, it was also partial and incomplete. Women from certain countries remained underrepresented as Olympians. Those who did make it to the Olympic stage were often sexualized. Women also did not achieve gender parity in leadership or coaching positions.

The conclusion charts women's progress and setbacks at the beginning of the twenty-first century. Though women competed in an equal number of sports by the 2008 Beijing Summer Olympics, they participated in fewer events than male Olympians and remained underrepresented as athletes, coaches, and leaders.[6] The IOC sought to combat gender inequities by approving a new strategic plan in 2014, the Olympic Agenda 2020. It included forty recommendations, one of which called for 50 percent female participation by the 2020 Tokyo Olympics. To help achieve this goal, the IOC also approved the IOC Gender Equality Review Project in 2018. The document outlined ways to improve gender equity in several areas, including sport participation, media portrayal, governance structure, and funding.[7] Women made some strides as a result; they achieved near parity in participation but fell short of equality in leadership. In addition, expanded opportunities sparked questions about eligibility. The IOC outlined various policies for intersex and transgender athletes during the first two decades of the century. After implementing restrictions for both groups centered on hormone levels, the IOC introduced a new policy in 2021 that sought to rectify the harms caused by past sex verification practices. It encouraged sport leaders to prioritize inclusion and move away from suspicion-based, laboratory testing. As a result, federations instituted a range of policies for intersex and trans athletes, from unmediated inclusion to outright bans.

This pocketbook offers details about important milestones

in Olympic history and illustrates the salient themes that have shaped women's involvement in the Games since the beginning. Coubertin envisioned his sporting forum as a place for masculine excellence. In many ways, the Games are still "haunted by the ghost" of Coubertin and his "patriarchal ideology." [8] Throughout the history of the Olympics women have continuously fought for increased opportunities as athletes, equal access to elite sports, and a place in the decision-making process. Yet equality in all spheres of the Olympic Movement remains unachieved.

CHAPTER 1

Obstacles to Women's Participation in Sport

Women's Olympic Milestones, 1896-1916

1896 — Women do not officially compete at the inaugural modern Olympic Games. Greek runner Stamata Revithi unofficially runs the Olympic marathon course from Marathon to Athens.

22 women (975 men) compete at the Paris Olympics for the first time. Women from Bohemia, France, Great Britain, Italy, Switzerland, and the United States participate.[1]

1900 — Swiss Olympian Hélène de Pourtalès is the first woman to win a gold medal at the Olympics. She is part of the winning sailing team.

Great British tennis player Charlotte Cooper is the first woman to win an individual Olympic event.

US golfer Margaret Abbott is the second woman to win an individual Olympic event. Abbott receives a porcelain bowl instead of a medal.

Women's Olympic Milestones, 1896-1916, continued...

1904	6 women (645 men) compete at the St. Louis Olympics.
	US archers Matilda Howell, Emma Cooke, and Eliza Pollock finish first, second, and third in the two individual archery events open to women.
1906	12 Danish female gymnasts perform at the Intercalated Games in Athens, Greece.
1908	37 women (1,971 men) compete at the London Olympics. The number of female Olympians increases to seventy-one when participants in ice-skating and demonstration sports are included. Women from Germany and Sweden participate for the first time.
	Great British figure skater Madge Syers wins the inaugural women's singles event.
	Swedish swimmer Ebba Gisico and six Icelandic sportswomen give demonstrations of diving and swimming, and twenty Danish athletes display gymnastics, on the very first day of the London Games.
1912	47 women (2,359 men) compete at the Stockholm Olympics. Women from Australasia, Austria, Belgium, Denmark, Finland, and Norway participate for the first time.
	Diving and swimming debut. Women compete in the 10m platform, 100m freestyle, and 4 x 100m freestyle relay.

Women's Olympic Milestones, 1896-1916, continued...

1912 Swedish diver Greta Johansson is the first woman to win an Olympic diving medal. Australian swimmer Fanny Durack is the first woman to win an individual Olympic swimming medal. Great Britain wins the first women's Olympic relay medal.

1916 The Berlin Olympics are canceled due to the outbreak of World War I.

This first chapter covers the early history of women's participation in sport. This history spans more than three thousand years and is focused on Western Europe as the cradle of modern competitive sport and the Olympic Games. A major theme of this chapter is how the social roles ascribed to women significantly hindered their opportunities to take part in various forms of physical activity. From ancient times to the first editions of the modern Olympics, sport leaders' beliefs about women's inferiority limited their engagement in competitions.

Women's Early Involvement in Sport

Women have always participated in sport and physical activities. Early records in the form of ceramic female ballplayer figures provide hints that women engaged in ball games in Mesoamerica during the early classic period (250 – 900 CE).[2] Similarly, women were physically active in early Chinese societies (3000 BCE – 476 BCE), in which cooperation and harmony, rather than competition, were emphasized.[3] In several texts from

Greek mythology, women participate in competitions and play games, too. For example, Homer writes in his epic poem *Odyssey* (written around 800 BCE) about Nausicaa, who plays ball with her maidens.[4]

Yet, in most early societies, women's possibilities to participate in physical activity were limited due to their subordinate roles in communities ruled by men. This also explains why scholars have less historical sources about women from early periods. The most compelling sources of early forms of physical activity are from Greek antiquity, which has the largest impact on modern day understandings of sport. The ancient Greek sport festivals also displayed patriarchal power, but were in fact very different from today's "sport." These festivals were extremely violent and composed entirely of individual competitions.[5] Even though the available sources reveal little about the role of women in ancient Greek society, it is evident that women had considerably less rights than men. In Athens, women were not allowed to vote or own land. Whereas men were permitted to appear in public life, engage in politics, or participate in cultural events, women's place was generally considered to be in the home. There, a woman's main task was to manage the household and bear children.

Such social expectations for women also impacted their lack of participation in ancient Greek sporting events. For example, there are very few records of women competing at the Ancient Olympic Games of Greek antiquity, held between 776 BCE and 393 CE. The Olympic Games were a series of sporting competitions, held every four years in the Sanctuary of Olympia in Elis, Greece, in honor of Zeus, the king of the gods. They were part of the four sporting festivals of the Panhellenic Games. Much more is known and has been written about the competitions between men, who competed naked to demonstrate their physique and athleticism to Zeus.

Married women were likely not allowed to attend the Olympic Games at all, probably due to cultic reasons.[6] However, a few writings, mainly by Greek geographer Pausanias, offer insights into women's activities. He described how some women defied laws and social expectations by attending the games. Pausanias also sheds light on the only known running competition for women in Greek antiquity. He reports that separate games for girls, named the Heraean Games in honor of Greek goddess Hera, were also held at Olympia.[7] Pausanias argued that they were founded to celebrate the marriage of the Queen of Pisa, Hippodamia, to Pelops. The Heraean Games consisted only of stadium runs by competitors of different age groups.[8] The existing information on the ancient Greek sporting competitions therefore describes the limited participation of women, which mostly likely occurred in separated events. Yet, considering that the Ancient Olympic Games lasted for over twelve centuries, historians assume that significant changes occurred over time.

Because women similarly had minimal involvement in politics or public life in ancient Rome, few sources discuss their participation in physical activities. It is nevertheless clear that class differences determined whatever limited opportunities did exist. Upper-class women in the Roman Empire had personal freedoms and could attend entertainment events, such as the increasingly spectacular gladiator combats and chariot races. Men and women sat together, in contrast to the segregated habits of Greek customs.[9] There is also evidence that upper-class women engaged in athletic activities. A mosaic in a Roman villa from the fourth or fifth century displays nine women with different types of balls and dumbbells. Women might have also competed as gladiators, but the existing sources focus primarily on male gladiators.

In Europe, differences in sport participation across class lines, both for men and women, heightened during the Middle Ages (around 400 to late fourteenth century), the Renaissance (around the fifteenth century to 1650), and the Enlightenment periods (around 1650 to 1780). Though the Middle Ages cover more than a thousand years, two basic means of labor for men persisted throughout the period: fighting as a soldier, either independently or for a king, or working as a peasant or serf. Women's responsibilities again largely remained reduced to household activities.

Soldiers engaged in sporting activities designed to improve their fighting skills, such as mock combat fights or jousting. Men demonstrated these skills in Middle Age tournaments against other knights while members of the ruling class, male and female, watched. Over time, women took on increasingly important roles in organizing the knights' tournaments, such as the staging and execution of the spectacles.[10] Men also occasionally allowed women of nobility to participate in their hunting activities.

In contrast, peasant women were mainly reduced to the role of spectators well into the Renaissance period. Women could take part in foot races and folk football games, primarily during the festive season. For example, organizers of the local Cotswold Games, which started in 1612 in the Cotswold region of England, brought the different classes together and allowed men and women to participate. Men and women ran, wrestled, and danced together.[11] In other parts of Europe, women participated in ball games, boat races, foot races, and horse races.

When educational reformers in continental Europe started to attach different forms of educational meaning to gymnastics at the end of the eighteenth century, they focused on young men. For example, the German educator Johann GutsMuths introduced physical exercise into the German school curriculum, but only for boys. Similarly, the inventor of German gymnastics, Ludwig Jahn, who founded the first gymnastics facilities, initially restricted access to boys and men. Similar patterns developed in France and England. In England, the connection of physical activity to education provided the impetus for the development of modern sport, the focus of the next section.

In summary, this brief overview shows that social constraints imposed by men fostered women's lack of sport participation. This occurred across both geographical areas and time periods. Class and gender were significant determinants of whether individuals could freely engage in physical activity. The upper class could participate before the lower class, men could participate before women, and upper-class women could participate before lower-class women. Men often justified women's exclusion by pointing to the use of physical activities for military purposes. They also attached values typically associated with men, such as physical strength, competition, discipline, and toughness, to such endeavors. This only increased when educators attached similar values to sport.

Made by Men for Men: The Origins of Modern Sport

Several forms of "modern sport," characterized by competitiveness, standardized rules, and bureaucratic structures, originated in Western countries throughout the nineteenth century, specifically in Great Britain. Historian Allen Guttmann argues that increased standardization and measurement, essential features of the industrialization, characterized the shift from pre-modern activities to modern sport. Baseball, boxing, cricket, foot races, and horse races all became increasingly rationale and organized from the second half of the eighteenth century onwards.[12] For example, the Knickerbocker Baseball Club in the United States outlined a constitution and drew up rules for the sport in 1845. Yet, as in the preceding periods with pre-modern physical activities, men primarily engaged in modern sport.

Schoolmasters at British public schools, private boarding schools for upper-class boys, embraced the emerging forms of modern sport as a means for "character building," starting in the middle of the nineteenth century. At elite schools, such as those located in the English towns Rugby and Eton, teachers allowed pupils to engage in self-organized team sports. This led boys to create early forms of rugby (derived from the name of the town) and football (soccer). Many public school boys became so obsessed with the sporting activities that they established sport clubs, leagues, and federations to organize competitive sport outside the school setting. In this way, graduates of British public schools formed the key constituents of the modern day sport system. Table 1.1 provides an overview of milestones in organized men's sport.

Table 1.1: Nineteenth Century Milestones of Organized Men's Sport

1829: First organized boat race between Oxford and Cambridge

1844: First international sporting competition: cricket match between Canada and the United States

1845: First formalized baseball rules outlined

1863: First national governing body of a sport founded, the Football Association in London

1872: First international football (soccer) match between England and Scotland

1876: First national baseball league starts in the United States

1877: First international cricket test match between Australia and England

> **1881:** Federation of International Gymnastics founded
>
> **1887:** First edition of the US national tennis championships contended (forerunner of the US Open)
>
> **1888:** First football (soccer) league in England founded
>
> **1891:** Basketball invented by US physical educator James Naismith
>
> **1896:** First modern Olympic Games held in Athens, Greece

Significantly, the emergence of sport from the public schools bolstered ideas about athletic masculinity. In his 1857 bestselling novel *Tom Brown's Schooldays*, author Thomas Hughes advocated for schoolboys' participation in sport.[13] He suggested it increased physical and mental toughness as education through sport was a way to "masculinize" boys. Concerns that the rapidly increasing urbanization and industrialization endangered the dominant role of men stirred these beliefs.[14] As a result, leaders in different sectors, including in business, education, military, and politics—often themselves public school graduates—promoted sporting activities as masculine activities. Their ideas spread through the British Empire and resulted in the establishment of similar sport ideals in different parts of the world. For example, British administrators promoted cricket in Indian and other South Asian countries, casting the seeds for today's popularity of the sport in the region.[15]

Fears that upper-class men lacked masculinity also emerged in the United States in the nineteenth century. Increased industrialization, immigration, and urbanization, along with women's demands for suffrage, sparked fears about the place of men in society. Like in Britain, people in the US believed that participation in "manly" sport activities provided men with the possibility to strengthen their masculinity.[16] This made sport more acceptable and helped it spread around the country.

Class continued to be a determining factor in sport participation. In the United States and Great Britain, a new middle-class emerged in the second half of the nineteenth century with increased leisure time and disposable income. People turned to sports to spend their free time and their money, as spectators and participants. Yet, middle-class participants, led by the public-school graduates, worried about participating against—and potentially losing to— the working class. To bar working-class athletes, they created amateurism rules. Amateurism rules limited participation to those who could engage in sport without compensation. It ensured only the wealthy, those who could afford to compete without a paycheck, could participate. Middle-class sport leaders created organizations to oversee compliance with this rule. Because working-class athletes could not compete without financial support, they created their own sports movements that permitted professionalism.

Class tensions similarly influenced women's participation. Upper-class women participated in "lady-like" activities, those that required money and exhibited grace, such as horse riding, croquet, golf, and tennis. Those sports were also considered to require only lowered, acceptable forms of physical effort. For example, women first competed at Wimbledon in 1884, seven years after the tournament debuted. However, as sport historian Jaime Schultz attests, their involvement was more for social than physical reasons.[17] Women had to adhere to the existing social norms. For example, they had to wear long, white, and highly impractical dresses while competing.

Obstacles to Women's Participation in Sport

1884 Wimbledon Winner, Maud Watson of Great Britain.
Wikimedia Commons.

The realities for working-class women differed significantly from those of their upper-class counterparts. They had to perform physical labor, oftentimes outside of the home, which limited their time for leisure activities.[18] However, in contrast to previous times, women in Great Britain did watch some working-class sports, such as football (soccer). They received mixed reactions as spectators as some opponents considered it inappropriate.[19]

In New Zealand and South Africa, two countries connected to the British Empire where British sporting inventions had spread, sport leaders rejected women's involvement entirely. Women therefore participated more informally, locally, and separately. Such "hidden" involvement was a consequence of the male control of the sanctioned sporting space.[20] Men felt threatened by emerging women's movements and considered sport their way to display masculinity.

The idea of separate spheres, in which men oversaw the public and women oversaw the private realms, shaped peoples' inclusion in and exclusion from modern sport. Whereas separate spheres ideology attributed competitiveness, performance, movement, and dynamics to men, it characterized women as quiet, passive, and focused on maternal care. Many people believed that women would become "masculinized" by engaging in grueling sporting activities. For example, when watching a cycling competition at the end of the nineteenth century, a spectator asked with concern, "Can we admire a girl, however beautiful she may be, whose face is as red as a lobster, and streaming with perspiration, whose hair is hanging in a mop about her ears . . . , and whose general appearance is dusty, untidy, and unwomanly."[21] Such sentiments portrayed women's engagement in physical activities as a breach of feminine norms.

In contrast, men—who dominated public life by holding the highest positions in politics, the military, education, and medicine—expressed less reluctance about women participating in certain "feminine" sports, such as gymnastics and dance. Such activities were believed to support forms of expression associated with femininity and allowed men to ensure that only boys and men were masculinized through sport.

As a result, sport organizers commonly used medical claims to justify keeping women sidelined. Late nineteenth and early twentieth century mainstream medical ideals suggested that women suffered from long-term health consequences when "exceeding their natural limits" through participation in competitive physical activities. Assuming that women, in contrast to men, possessed only limited amounts of energy, medical doctors feared that sports participation harmed women's reproductive capabilities. In the elite circles of the nineteenth-century United States, the idea that sport was a threat to white women's fertility was commonplace.[22] If one followed this argument, and most men and women did at the time, white middle-class women could not engage in any competitive sport due to health reasons. This prevented them from participating in any activities that required strength, contact, or endurance. Women who did not follow the medical guidelines faced accusations that they threatened the future of the entire human race, as many people at the time believed that white women's ultimate purpose was the bearing and upbringing of children. These ideas transcended class and geographic areas. For example, working-class women in the United Kingdom who played football (soccer) were often stigmatized and ridiculed.[23] However, medical ideas about female fragility did not include Black women in the United States. Racist sentiments connected to slavery suggested Black women were more equipped for physical labor than white women. But Black women were nevertheless also excluded from US sport. Racist customs and laws required racial segregation, denying Black athletes opportunities in organized sport.

Based on these faulty medical beliefs, many male-led governing bodies of sport refused to organize competitions for women. Women therefore established their own clubs, organizations, and competitions. For example, English golfer Issette Pearson helped found the Ladies' Golf Union in 1893 as the governing body for girls' and women's amateur golf in England, Ireland, Scotland, and Wales. In the United States, physical educator

Senda Berenson introduced women's basketball at Smith College in 1892.[24] These organizations and clubs were primarily open for upper-class women only. Female organizers also embraced the concept of moderation, modifying the men's version of the sport to make it more appropriate for girls and women. For example, Berenson divided the basketball court into three sections so her students would not risk running the length of the floor. Yet, despite widespread resistance to their participation, women competed in various events. Table 1.2 provides an overview of milestones in organized women's sport in Great Britain and the United States.

Table 1.2: Nineteenth Century Milestones of Organized Women's Sport in Great Britain and the United States

1811: First women's golf tournament organized in Great Britain

1875: First official baseball game between women in Illinois, United States

1884: Women compete for the first time at the Wimbledon tennis tournament

1886: All English Women's Hockey Association established

1887: Women compete for the first time at the US Open in tennis

1892: Women's basketball introduced at Smith College by Senda Berenson

1893: Ladies' Golf Union founded in St. Andrews, Great Britain

1896: First intercollegiate women's basketball game between UCLA and Stanford

In summary, class and gender ideas shaped the emergence of modern sport. Sport organizations and rules served upper-class men. As sport scholar Jennifer Hargreaves notes, the "use of the physical body was very much constrained by the social body," with the ruling men demanding that the "lower" classes and the "lower" gender subordinate to their ideas.[25] Male organizers constructed sports in a way that separated men's and women's supposed innate characters and capacities.[26] In other words, the men who had invented sports in the nineteenth century ensured that only boys and men could demonstrate competitiveness, strength, and power.

The Exclusion of Women from the Early Olympic Games

French aristocrat Pierre de Coubertin founded the modern Olympic Games, first held in Athens, Greece, in 1896. Ancient sport and the English sporting traditions, discussed in the previous sections, shaped Coubertin's ideas about the Olympic Movement. After reading extensively about ancient Greece, Coubertin learned about the Greek belief in the harmony of body, mind, and soul.[27] While he appreciated this view of humanity, he did not want to imitate the Ancient Games entirely. Instead, from watching sporting activities at various public schools in England, Coubertin learned how the values attached to the individual sporting experiences could be extended to other facets of life. He admired the ideas in *Tom Brown's Schooldays*, which he read in French as a young schoolboy. As a result, Coubertin meshed the two ideals together in his blueprint for an international sporting event.

As described in the previous section, ancient Greek and English cultures promoted masculinity through sport, and this appealed to Coubertin for two major reasons. First, in his youth, Coubertin had been traumatized by the loss of France against Germany in the Franco-Prussian War of 1870-71. He believed that the German soldiers' involvement in gymnastics activities ("Turnen") fostered their military superiority. Similarly, he had witnessed the power of the British Empire and concluded that British boys' involvement in sporting activities contributed to their soldierly capabilities. Coubertin therefore thought that French boys and men should engage in physical activity to enhance their masculinity and improve their bodily capacities. Second, Coubertin was a man of his time. He was convinced that a woman should limit herself to household matters and assume a passive role in society. In 1901, Coubertin noted that, "The role of women in the world remains what it has always been. She is above all the companion of man, the future mother of a family, and she should be brought up with this fixed destiny in mind."[28] Against this background, it is not surprising that Coubertin did not foresee a place for women in his Olympic project.

During an 1894 congress at the Sorbonne University in Paris, Coubertin initiated the foundation of the modern Olympic Games. Originally, Coubertin, as secretary-general of the Union of French Sports Associations, invited delegates—all male—to discuss amateurism. He later changed the purpose and title of the event to the "Congress on the Revival of the Olympic Games."[29] Coubertin presented his Olympic idea to delegates from French and foreign sport organizations and clubs. They consequently adopted a resolution to stage the first Olympic Games in 1896.

Delegates decided that Athens would host the event, even though the French baron had preferred Paris as the first host city. Coubertin had compromised amidst pressure from Greek and British sport officials, who had also wanted to organize the first Olympic Games. The Congress participants also agreed on a first international definition of amateurism—one that banned any athlete who earned money through sport—and founded the International Olympic Committee (IOC). Coubertin handpicked the initial IOC members, all men, which is unsurprising given the lack of female leaders in sport organizations at this time. Though the newly formed IOC neither outlined specific rules that excluded women from becoming IOC members nor explicitly prevented their participation in the Olympics, it appears that the delegates never considered women's involvement.[30] The decision-making upper-class men simply assumed that women would not participate.

2nd IOC Session in Athens, 1896 – Group photograph of the members. Sitting: Pierre de Coubertin, IOC Secretary General; Demetrius Vikelas, IOC Pdt; and Aleksey Dimitrievic Boutowski, IOC member (RUS). Standing: IOC members : Karl August Willibald Gebhardt (GER), Jiri Guth-Jarkovsky (BOH), Ferenc Kemeny (HUN), and Viktor Black (SWE). Courtesy of the International Olympic Committee.

Men competed in several individual sports at the inaugural Games in 1896: cycling, fencing, gymnastics, sailing/rowing, shooting, swimming, tennis, track and field, weightlifting, and wrestling. While Coubertin contributed much to the international dissemination of British masculinity ideals, he did not embrace British affinity for team sports. He favored individual sports for the Olympics, believing they highlighted manliness and pure physical efforts.[31] Moreover, even though Coubertin himself played only a small role in the organization of the event, organizers did not invite women. Not a single woman officially competed at the Athens Olympics; however, evidence suggests that Stamata Revithi, a Greek woman and mother of three, ran the complete marathon distance a day prior to the official event.[32]

The French baron remained steadfast in his opposition to women's participation in competitive sport until his death in 1937.[33] In 1912, after women had officially participated in several Games, Coubertin voted against their inclusion, arguing that "the Olympic Games must be reserved for men."[34] He justified his opinion with a range of arguments. Coubertin thought that the inclusion of women would lead to organizational difficulties for host cities. Further, he agreed with those voicing aesthetical and physical concerns if women's competitions were held alongside men's competitions, infamously arguing: "this feminine semi-Olympiad is impractical, uninteresting, ungainly, and I do not hesitate to add, improper."[35] These beliefs mirrored the attitudes of the men from the aristocracy.[36] Yet, as we will see in the next section, Coubertin was unable to prevent women from participating in the Olympic Games entirely.

Women's Olympic Debut

Women officially competed for the first time at the 1900 Olympic Games in Paris, France, and four years later in St. Louis, United States. Coubertin and the IOC again did not actively include women's competitions. Rather, as was the case in Athens in 1896, the organizing committees of the host cities set up the Olympic programme. Because the 1900 and 1904 Games were organized jointly with World Fairs, organizers staged the sporting events in a disjointed manner. They viewed sports as sideshows to the main event, the World Fair exhibitions. Coubertin also lost control over his Olympic project—including over the specific participants he had in mind. Institutional stakeholders, such as International Federations and National Olympic Committees, which became crucial in the writing of Olympic participation rules throughout the twentieth century, later gained power to influence the staging of the Games.

Local groups therefore ushered in women's participation. For the 1900 Paris Olympic Games, a small organizing committee oversaw the staging of the sporting competitions. This committee, in turn, delegated the responsibility of inviting athletes to local Parisian sport clubs. They extended invitations for participation in tennis and golf, two events viewed as appropriate for women's involvement. Parisian clubs—without a clear rule that allowed or disallowed female participation—extended invitations to both men and women.[37] Eighteen women consequently competed in the first individual women's competitions in tennis and golf. They participated in long dresses in a way that conformed to the social norms of the time. Four more women competed in team events, amongst them the first female Olympic champion, Hélene de Pourtalès from Switzerland, who was part of a winning sailing crew.

Women who competed at the 1900 Paris Olympic Games came from the upper class. Pourtalès, for example, was married to the aristocrat Count Hermann Alexander de Pourtalès, who was on the winning boat with his wife. Working-class women had little time to engage in physical activities and those few who earned money through sport, for example as physical education teachers, were barred through the IOC's amateur rules.

Paris 1900 Olympic Games, Golf Women - Two competitors next to the same hole. Courtesy of the International Olympic Committee.

For the 1904 St. Louis Olympics, Coubertin again had no influence over the participants. Stretched over several months, the Games were integrated in a world exhibition with an organizing committee independent from the IOC. This body called all competitive physical occurrences "Olympic events," making it difficult for Olympic historians to distinguish between proper sporting competitions and demonstration activities held for fun. The unclear status of competitions blurs the exact number of female Olympians at the 1904 Olympic Games. On the one hand, the official report of the Olympics makes no mention of female competitors, even in tennis and golf. On the other, historians have verified that six women competed in archery. Women had been members of the National Archery Association in the United States since 1879, and the competitions in St. Louis in 1904 served as the National Championships in the sport. As was the case of the women's events in Paris, the national context explains the women's involvement.

The Olympic Movement reached an unintended milestone in

1906. Following the success of the 1896 Athens Olympic Games, Greek organizers wanted to stage the Olympic Games in Greece on a regular basis. This countered Coubertin's plan for internationalization and his intention to award the Games to cities around the world. Coubertin therefore proposed that the Greek sport leaders stage "Intercalated Games," to be held in between the Olympic Games. Due to financial reasons, Greek organizers were not able to hold the event in 1898 or 1902, but did hold the first "Intercalated Games" in 1906. Although he initially proposed the idea, Coubertin came to view the Intercalated Games as in competition with the Olympics. Therefore, he did not attend and the IOC never recognized them as official Olympic Games. That said, the Intercalated Games played an important role in the survival of Coubertin's Olympics. For the first time since the inaugural Games in 1896, the sporting competitions were held in a well-organized (had its own organizing committee), compact (held over two weeks), independent (not connected to the World Fair), and international (twenty nations participated) manner. As a result, the Intercalated Games refocused attention on the Olympic Movement.[38] Women participated in tennis at the 1906 Intercalated Games, providing further evidence that male organizers considered the sport appropriate for upper-class women. Additionally, a group of twelve Danish female gymnasts, on invitation of the Greek royal family, took center stage at one point during the event. They became the first female performers in an Olympic stadium. Women's gymnastics had developed in Denmark during the late nineteenth century and the gymnasts performed synchronized movements for the audience.[39] Though the Danish gymnasts' appearance is a milestone in (unofficial) Olympic history, the ensuing media reports provided conflicting accounts. Some writers highlighted the femininity of the women's performance. According to one report, graceful movements, not athleticism, was "a way that our beautiful sex can take part in the competition at the next Olympic Games."

These accounts suggested women's beauty mattered more than their physical accomplishments. Yet, other reports suggested gymnastics could contribute to women's emancipation. Local writers suggested that "that the Danish women gymnasts' performance will possibly be the beginning of a revolution in the Greek people's idea of what a woman can and should be occupied with."[40] Taken together, the commentary illustrates the dueling ideas about elite sport for women.

Following Games that were folded into world exhibitions, the 1908 London Olympics was a stand-alone sporting forum. And while Coubertin maintained his concerns—though not active opposition—about women's participation, he had little room to maneuver since the organization of the Olympics continued to fall largely in the hands of the local organizing committees. Women thus increasingly participated in the Games. Thirty-seven women participated in four different sports: archery, figure skating, sailing (in mixed teams), and tennis. As before, these were sports largely interpreted as appropriate for upper-class women. Four years later in Stockholm, organizers added swimming to the programme and dropped archery. Women's gymnastics demonstrations by Scandinavian teams continued at both Games, and the sports that appeared on the programme for women mirrored those practiced by women in the country. British women competed in archery, skating, and tennis; Swedish women competed in diving, swimming, and tennis. The Swedish organizing committee also actively advocated for women's events. As recorded in the 1911 IOC meeting minutes, "[The Swedes] are also feminists and women already admitted to the trials of lawn tennis and gymnastics exhibitions will be without a doubt in the swimming championships of 1912."[41] Because Swedish sport leaders more openly permitted women's swimming in the country, the Swedish organizing committees took on a decisive role in allowing women's events at the 1912 Olympics.[42]

The introduction of women's swimming into the Olympics was not without controversy, however. Swimming had been an Olympic discipline since 1896 but was restricted to men. Representatives from Belgium, Denmark, Finland, France, Germany, Great Britain, Hungary, and Sweden formed the International Swimming Federation (FINA) in 1908. Some of the countries originally involved in the foundation of FINA more readily accepted women in the water. They considered swimming suitable for women: the in-water movements were barely seen, swimming took place in closed spaces, and medical studies highlighted the health benefits of mild swimming exercises.[43] In contrast, French and US sport leaders prohibited their female athletes from competing in Olympic swimming. Concerns about decency and modesty laws, which prevented women from showing their arms and legs in public, outlawed their participation.

Women therefore did participate in the early editions of the Olympic Games, but only in a few selected sports. See table 1.3 for an overview of the number of women at each Olympics and the sports in which they participated. The local organizing committees made women's involvement possible; however, they limited female inclusion to events practiced by upper-class women that focused on beauty and grace.[44] Unlike the IOC members who ignored women entirely, local organizers recognized that women already competed in sport. The fact that four entirely separate host committees admitted women to the Games shows that male organizers accepted *some* women's sports, at least to a certain degree.[45] Nevertheless, though Coubertin did not implement an explicit rule against women's events at the Olympics through his IOC, he remained steadfast in his opposition to their participation.

Table 1.3: Official Women's Participation at Olympic Games Prior to World War One

Year	Host City	Women	Men	Women's Individual Competitions
1896	Athens	0	241	-
1900	Paris	22	975	Golf, Tennis
1904	St. Louis	6	645	Archery
1908	London	37	1,971	Archery, Skating, Tennis
1912	Stockholm	47	2,359	Diving, Simming, Tennis

Conclusion

A few themes emerge from this overview of women's early participation in physical activities, sport, and the early editions of the Olympic Games. First, while women have always participated in physical activities, their involvement was limited due to ideas about their supposedly inferior role in ancient and early modern societies. Second, when men "invented" modern sport during the nineteenth century, they conceived it as an exclusively male endeavor. Initially considered a replacement for military activities and later used for educational purposes, sport became a space to cultivate masculinity. Men brought forward medical, aesthetic, and social reasons to justify the exclusion of women from sports. Participation in activities associated with upper-class femininity, such as golf and tennis, were more widely accepted.

Third, despite men's opposition, women did compete. They founded their own sport clubs and organizations. Yet because working-class women did not have time for leisure activities, female involvement in sport was initially limited to the upper class. Strict interpretations of amateurism hampered working-class women's involvement. Finally, the founder of the modern Olympics, Pierre de Coubertin, vigorously opposed the inclusion of women in competitive sport throughout his entire life. Women gained admission to the early editions of the Games against his wishes, because the local organizing committees added them. In contrast to Coubertin, organizing committees recognized that some, mainly upper-class, women participated in organized sport and allowed them to compete at the Olympics.

Discussion Questions

- How did men justify excluding women from the emerging sporting practices in the second half of the nineteenth century?

- In what ways did women engage in physical activities and sports?

- Would women have been better off creating their own separate organizations and Olympic Games? What would have been the advantages of a separate Olympics? Disadvantages?

- How did women gain inclusion into the Olympics? What were the limitations of this approach?

CHAPTER 2

Fights for Inclusion

Women's Olympic Milestones, 1920-1944

1920
65 women (2,562 men) compete at the Antwerp Olympics. Women from Australia, Czechoslovakia, New Zealand, the Netherlands, and South Africa participate for the first time.

US women compete in Olympic swimming for the first team. The team sweeps the competition in the two individual events and finish first in the relay.

1921
The *1er Meeting International d'Education Physique Féminine de Sports Athlétiques,* "Women's Olympiad," takes place in Monaco. Approximately 100 women from four countries compete in ten track and field events, as well as in exhibitions in basketball, gymnastics, pushball, and rhythmic gymnastics.

1922
The first *Jeux Athlétiques Internationaux Féminins,* "Women's Olympics," takes place in Paris. Seventy-five women from five countries compete in eleven track and field events.

Women's Olympic Milestones, 1920-1944, continued...

1924

The first Winter Olympics are held in Chamonix, France. Eleven women compete in figure skating, the only sport open for women. Austrian skater Herma Szabo is the first female Winter Olympic champion.

Figure skater Cecil Eustace Smith is the first woman from Canada at the Olympics.

135 women (2,954 men) compete at the Paris Summer Olympics. Women from Greece, Hungary, India, Ireland, Luxembourg, Poland, and Spain participate for the first time.

Danish fencer Ellen Osiier wins the gold medal in the individual foil, the first fencing event open to women. Thirteen women compete in "ladies singles" and pairs.

1928

26 women (438 men) compete at the St. Moritz Winter Olympics.

Thirteen-year-old Norwegian skater Sonja Henie wins the gold medal at the St. Moritz Games. She defends her title again in 1932 and 1936.

277 women (2,606 men) compete at the Amsterdam Summer Olympics. Women from Japan, Latvia, Lithuania, and Romania participate for the first time.

Women's Olympic Milestones, 1920-1944, continued...

1928

Women compete in five track and field events for the first time at the Summer Olympics, setting world records in the 800m, 4 x 100m relay, discus throw, and high jump.

Japanese runner Hitomi Kinue is the first Asian woman to win an Olympic medal in the 800m.

Concerns that women "collapsed" at the conclusion of the 1928 800m convince IOC leaders to prohibit women from competing in distances longer than 200m until 1960.

21 women (231 men) compete at the Lake Place Winter Olympics.

126 women (1,206 men) compete at the Los Angeles Summer Olympics. Women from Brazil, Guatemala, and Mexico participate for the first time.

1932

US athlete Mildred "Babe" Didrikson wins two gold medals in the 80m hurdles and javelin throw, and one silver medal in the high jump.

US swimmer Eleanor G. Holm wins the gold medal in the 100m backstroke. She is later expelled from the 1936 Olympic team for drinking champagne at a party aboard a ship on the way to the Berlin Games.

Women's Olympic Milestones, 1920-1944, continued...

	80 women (566 men) compete at the Garmisch-Partenkirchen Winter Olympics. Alpine skier Karin Peckert-Forsmann is the first woman from Estonia at the Olympics.
1936	331 women (3,632 men) compete at the 1936 Berlin Olympics. Women from Argentina, Chile, China, Turkey, and Yugoslavia participate for the first time.
	Japanese swimmer Hideko Maehata is the first Asian woman to win a gold medal in the 200m breaststroke.
	Runner Tidye Pickett is the first Black woman from the United States to compete at the Olympics.
1940	The Tokyo Olympics are canceled due to the Second World War.
1944	The London Olympics are canceled due to the Second World War.

Chapter 2 explores the tensions between women's sport organizations and Olympic institutions during the interwar period (1918-1939). Male Olympic leaders continued to strongly oppose extensive women's participation in this period, during which five editions of the Summer Olympic Games and the creation of the Winter Olympic Games occurred. In contrast to early Games, for which local organizing committees decided upon admission to the competitions, the all-male International Olympic Committee (IOC) and International Sport Federations (IFs) increasingly took control of who could and could not participate. The men in charge limited female Olympians to competitions that aligned with traditional gender roles and ideals, allowing them to participation in diving, figure skating, swimming, and tennis. Track and field, the most popular and important Olympic sport, remained off limits for women. In this vacuum, female organizers created separate forums for women to demonstrate their physical athleticism, which included the "Women's Olympics." The threat of female leadership over elite sport pushed the IOC and IFs to take control over women-led events, eventually leading to the demise of these sport organizations. Men thus retained control and continued to impose feminine body ideals in various ways, including through the introduction of mandatory, on-site sex controls.

The First World War as a Turning Point

Following the success of the 1908 and 1912 Olympic Games, the IOC awarded the right to host the 1916 event to Germany's capital, Berlin. In conversations about organizing the Berlin Olympics, the IOC again debated the question of women's involvement. During the 1914 Olympic Congress in Paris, Pierre de Coubertin proposed excluding women entirely, threatening to retire if he was outvoted. IOC members called his bluff. They continued to permit women's participation, but only in a handful of events.[1] Coubertin did not retire. Delegates did acquiesce to a different wish of the founder and rejected a proposal to introduce track and field for women, the core Olympic sport at the time.[2] These discussions foreshadowed the fight over women's track and field, which dominated much of the debate about their Olympic inclusion throughout the interwar years. The 1914 Congress also decreased the authority of the local organizing committees over the Olympic programme and admission of participants, leaving fewer possibilities for hosts to include women in Olympic events. Yet, the outbreak of the First World War halted the plans and caused the cancelation of the Berlin Games.

Those who opposed women's involvement in track and field deemed the sport too physical and masculine for women. They believed it threatened the feminine form, an attitude that prevailed throughout the entire interwar period. Medical concerns again shaped the discussions. According to sport historian Jennifer Hargreaves, the focus on dynamic and physical efforts in track and field led many medical experts to conclude that the sport harmed women's health and damaged the female physique, with particularly detrimental effects on reproduction.[3]

In stark contrast to the persistent, conventional gender ideals within the Olympic Movement, the First World War proved to be a pivotal event for women's participation in physical activity and sport. Many women assumed male occupations in the absence of men, who were recruited as soldiers and had left their homes for years, many never returning to their families. Regulated labor hours and permanent incomes allowed women more time and money to participate in leisure activities.

British football (soccer) provides an example of the changing norms. Because Britain stood at the forefront in the fight for women's suffrage, national leaders also more readily encouraged women's inclusion in sport. After performing demanding manual work, many women played football for enjoyment and female teams emerged all over the country. Some matches drew thousands of spectators and some female footballers gained celebrity status.[4] Though not all countries mirrored the British stance on women's rights, women gained new opportunities in sport across Europe. In Germany, women engaged in field handball to raise their spirits and improve their health.[5] Medical ideologies thereby shifted during the war. What was once considered damaging to women's wellbeing slowly became viewed as a way to improve their vigor.

Despite the expanded opportunities the war provided women, men maintained control of most sport organizations. Female advancement remained limited as male leaders "monopolized resources and held controlling and decision-making power."[6] For example, in Canada and the United States, women's participation in sport increased after the end of the War. However, the men's track and field organizations in both countries continued to prohibit female inclusion in the sport.[7]

Male administrators around the world regularly denied women access to elite sport. In response to repeated rejections, women increasingly established their own clubs, competitions, and federations.[8] The growing suffrage movements in Europe and North America provided additional support for these efforts. For example, the International Gymnastics Federation did not include women's gymnastics sections. In response, French women's sport advocates formed a separate organization for women's gymnastics, "Union Française de Gymnastique Féminine," in 1912. Supporters also formed three other women's sport clubs in Paris around this time, but their opinions on female competition differed, highlighting some of the complexities faced by women's groups at the time. People disagreed about appropriate clothing or separate women's competitions. Some demanded full emancipation while others outlined more careful approaches.[9]

The efforts of French feminist Alice Milliat were the most significant in regards to women's eventual participation in track and field at the Olympic Games. Born in Nantes, France, in 1884, Milliat lived in London for several years, where she became familiar with the women's movement in the country. A few years after her return to France in 1910, she joined Femina Sport (founded in 1912), France's first women's sports club and one of the three rivalling women's sport organizations mentioned above. In 1915, Milliat became the club's president. Amongst the different French women's sport organization, Femina Sport was the most progressive and members were encouraged to participate in "typically male" sports, such as football (soccer) and rugby.[10]

Alice Milliat, President of Femina Sport, in 1919.
Agence Meurisse. Wikimedia Commons.

Milliat was influential in helping the three women's sport organizations cooperate and organize the first national track and field championships for women in 1917. The event focused on track and field because the sport raised the most aesthetical and medical concerns for those who opposed women's inclusion. Although only a small stepping-stone, Milliat's persistence and preparedness to overcome conflicting opinions were evident in her success in staging the event. The three organizations then decided to create a new umbrella organization for women's track and field in France, the *Fédération des Sociétés Féminines Sportives de France*, the Federation of French Women's Sports Clubs (FSFSF). At first, men headed this organization, but again Milliat slowly managed to take control. In 1919, she became FSFSF president.

France was not the only country in which such developments took place. Similar processes occurred in other European countries. Women's track and field developed in Belgium, Czechoslovakia, Italy, Poland, Norway, and Switzerland during the War. In Austria, a women's track and field federation was founded in 1918, staging its own championships from 1918 onward. Though male-led, the German track and field federation encouraged sport clubs to allow women to participate and create separate women's sections. Many German women became active in these organizations in the early 1920s. However, due to Germany's role in the First World War, many foreign sport organizations barred German athletes from competing throughout much of the interwar era.

In summary, changes wrought by the First World War allowed women in Europe and North America to gain new freedoms. They increasingly took on manual labor and played important roles in securing the economic survival of their families. As a result, women participated more extensively in physical activities. The increasing number of women interested in sport required the organization of women's events. After the War, when men reassumed their traditional roles, debates about how to best organize women's competitions surfaced. Women established their own sport organizations, while men attempted to integrate them into the male-controlled, existing governing bodies.

Fights for Inclusion: Alice Milliat Challenges the Olympic Movement

Women's increased access to competitions occurred in line with larger women's rights movements of the early twentieth century. Women in Europe and North America successfully fought for voting rights, access to higher education, and freedom of movement. However, as in previous periods, class and geographical differences remained intact. The majority of women outside the upper classes in the Western world continued to experience legal, social, and political disadvantages.[11] The same held true in sport. Women in Western countries gained new sporting opportunities that were not achieved in other areas.

The fight for women's rights extended into sport during the interwar years, with Milliat at the forefront. In 1919, Milliat wrote a letter to Coubertin, asking for the admission of women into track and field events at the 1920 Antwerp Olympic Games, the first staged after the war.[12] Coubertin rejected the request. As a result, women competed in the same sports as they had eight years prior in Stockholm: in diving, swimming, and tennis, even though the number of participants rose to sixty-five women (compared to 2,562 men).

However, a few things had changed since the 1912 Olympic Games. As noted above, women participated in sport in much greater numbers. In addition, in Milliat and other French sport officials who promoted women's sport, the movement had a group of determined and capable leaders. These developments led to the first international women's sport competition, held in Monte Carlo, Monaco, in 1921. French sport officials organized the event to create attention for Monaco as a tourist destination, but also to promote women's sport. About one hundred participants from Great Britain, France, Italy, and Switzerland gathered to compete in various events. Some sources suggest athletes from Norway also participated, but they are not listed in the official result lists.

The majority of the events were in gymnastics and dance, but there were also ten track and field competitions. Exhibitions in basketball, gymnastics, pushball, and rhythmic gymnastics also took place, but were only considered part of the accompanying program. The marginalization of the track and field events angered Milliat and, as a result, she established her own sport federation, the *Fédération Sportive Féminine Internationale*, International Women's Sport Federation (FSFI), in October 1921. When founded, the FSFI consisted of delegates from twelve countries, making it the first international women's sport organization ever formed.[13] Moreover, the foundation of the FSFI firmly established Milliat as a leader and a pioneer for the international women's sport movement.

The foundation of the FSFI was also a response to the neglect of women's track and field by the men's governing body of the sport, the International Amateur Athletics Federation (IAAF).[14] The IAAF President, Swedish industrialist Sigfrid Edström, collaborated with IOC President Coubertin as an IOC Executive Board member. Edström was an important figure in the governance of the Olympic Movement for several decades. However, Edström's reason for fighting against women's track and field differed from that of the French baron. Whereas

Coubertin outright rejected women's sport in general, Edström was more concerned about the FSFI as a challenge to the IAAF's authority. The IAAF president did not want a second international track and field organization to exist.

The FSFI's success in staging international track and field events for women certainly provided Edström with reason to be concerned. In August 1922, Milliat organized the first "Women's Olympic Games," later called the first Women's World Games. Seventy-seven women from five countries competed in track and field in front of twenty thousand reported spectators. For the first time in an international women's sport competition, gymnastics and dance exhibitions that focused on grace and beauty were completely absent. The media description of the event was more positive than of previous international sporting events for women, even though newspapers continued to print negative comments. The FSFI continued to provide women a forum for international track and field. Table 2.1 shows the events in which women competed at the Women's World Games, from 1922-1934.

Table 2.1: FSFI Women's World Games

Year	Host City	No. of Countries	Addition of Track and Field Events
1922	Paris	5	60m, 100 yard race, 100 yard hurdles, 300m race, 1,000m race, 4x110 yard relay, high jump, javelin, long jump, standing long jump, and shot put
1926	Gothenburg	9	100m track walk, 250m race, and discus
1930	Prague	14	80m hurdles, 100m, 200m, 800m, 4x100m relay, and triathlon
1934	London	19	Pentathlon

Milliat's initiatives had two effects. First, her activism broke the male monopoly over the governance of sport. Female athletes were now able to demonstrate their athletic abilities to a broad audience. Second, her ability to stage an international competition for women allowed her to exert pressure on the established male-dominated sport organizations. She eventually used the FSFI's success as a bargaining chip in her later debates with male sport leaders, including Edström and Coubertin.

For the 1924 Paris Olympic Games, the IOC added women's fencing to the women's sport program. The addition of this largely aristocratic sport did not mean the IOC was ready to embrace more physical women's events, such as track and field or team sports.[15] In addition to the previously discussed aesthetic, social, and medical fears, the IOC grew concerned about organizational issues. Increased expenses convinced IOC members to resist expanding the Games. This provided them a welcomed excuse to avoid increasing women's involvement.[16] As a result, 135 women competed in diving, fencing, swimming, and tennis in 1924.

Along with limiting women's opportunities, the IOC claimed the word "Olympic" was its exclusive property. The IOC disliked the attachment of the "Olympic" label to the female sporting event, the "Women's Olympic Games." Male Olympic officials believed the women's use of the title diminished its value. Therefore, during the first "Women's Olympic Games" in 1922, the IOC President Coubertin and IAAF President Edström demanded Milliat drop the term from her competition. Edström also asked her to grant the IAAF the right to organize women's track and field.[17] Milliat denied both requests. She wanted all track and field events opened to women, not only a handful as Edström proposed. However, Milliat had to adopt a strategic stance and accepted a compromise to get women's track and field into the Olympics. She begrudgingly agreed to hand over the organization of women's track and field to the IAAF, but demanded the federation integrate FSFI representatives, including herself, into the IAAF's women's committee. The IAAF and the IOC agreed to include five track and field events for women at the 1928 Amsterdam Olympic Games. Women gained access to Olympic track and field, but the IAAF gained control over the entirety of the women's sport.

Although Milliat and the FSFI paved the way for international women's track and field events, not all women supported their endeavors. For example, some female sport administrators in the United States disapproved. When the IOC first announced the addition of the track and field events for 1928, the Committee on Women's Athletics, the National Association of Physical Education for College Women, and the Women's Division of the National Amateur Athletic Federation all opposed women's involvement.[18]

Despite such disapproval, the 1928 Amsterdam Olympic Games was a milestone in Olympic history. Female Olympians competed in track and field for the first time. As a direct result of Milliat's efforts, the IOC included the 100m, 800m, 4x100m relay, discus, and high jump. However, the significant progress for women's sport also provided fuel for continuing prejudices. Sensationalized reports emerged that "Eleven Wretched Women" collapsed at the end of the 800m race in complete exhaustion. Even though only nine Olympians participated in the race—with the top three finishing in world record time—and similar dramatics occurred in men's races, public outcry emerged.[19] The IOC voted in 1929 to drop all future female athletic events, using the "collapse" as proof that women were unfit for such physical endeavors. It backtracked from completely excluding women from track and field after facing pressure from US officials, and instead agreed to remove women's running events longer than

200m. This restriction remained in place for more than thirty years.

Amsterdam 1928 Olympic Games, Athletics, 800m Women - Final, Florence MacDonald (USA), Jean Thompson (CAN), Inga K. Gentzel (SWE) 3rd, Marie Döllinger (GER), Elfriede Wewer (GER), Fanny Rosenfeld (CAN), Karoline "Lina" Radke (GER) 1st, Gertruda Kilosowna (POL), and Kinue Hitomi (JPN) 2nd. Courtesy of the International Olympic Committee.

Somewhat surprisingly, IAAF President Edström also argued against the complete removal of women's track and field from the Olympics after the supposed collapse. His protest was not altruistic, however. Rather, he feared that if the IOC failed to sponsor women's events, Milliat would expand her independent efforts. Edström pointed out that Milliat was "trying with all her power to carry on her Games with a similar ritual as the Olympic Games," which could become "just as famous."[20] The IOC acquiesced and included six track and field events at the 1932 Los Angeles Games: the 80m hurdles, 100m, 4x100m relay, discus, javelin, and high jump. US athlete Mildred "Babe" Didrikson impressed the US crowd, winning gold medals in the 80m hurdles and javelin throw, and finishing second in the high jump. Didrikson became the only athlete to win individual Olympic medals in separate running, throwing, and jumping events. Equally impressively, she had earned a place on the Olympic team by single-handedly defeating an entire track and field team a few months before, at the Amateur Athletic Union national championship meet.[21]

Although the IOC had yielded and included women's track and field in Los Angeles, restrictions and gender separation remained in place. The organizing committee erected a temporary Olympic village to accommodate the athletes, but disallowed women from staying there, citing moral purposes. Instead, the committee housed women in a hotel. Concerns about the physical capabilities of women also remained, as did questions about which federation should control women's sport.

Milliat and the FSFI again successfully staged their World Games in 1930 and 1934; however, the 1930s saw the demise of the organization. The IAAF's grasp over women's track and field grew stronger throughout the decade. By 1936, Milliat was forced to disband the FSFI. The continuing opposition she received from the IAAF and economic factors forced her hand.[22] This marked the end of Milliat's fight for an independent sporting organization for women. She had to back down to the pressure from the IOC and the IAAF that perceived a separate women's sporting movement as dangerous to the success of the men's. The IOC and IAAF usurped the FSFI, forcing the women to give up their power. What started as a separatist movement ended up absorbed into the male sport organizations.

Milliat's campaign to get women's track and field into the Olympics proved to be a double-edged sword. She successfully pressured the IOC to accept women in running, jumping, and throwing events, from 1928 onwards. However, her compromise allowed President Edström and his colleagues to force the FSFI to fold into the IAAF—instead of merge—and slowly claim full control over women's track and field.

Continuing Concerns about Femininity

The institutional struggles to allow women to participate in track and field, the core sport of the Olympics, took place within the context of continuing concerns about femininity and women's bodies. Medical opinion throughout the 1920s and 1930s continued to suggest that excessive physical activity harmed women's reproductive capabilities.[23] The predominantly male medical profession believed that grueling competitions masculinized women, even though studies did not indicate any negative effects of sporting activities on them.[24] Medical experts nevertheless continued to highlight the physical differences between men and women, and argued against female involvement in competitive sport, further contributing to the marginalization of women's sport.

Race, class, and gender norms influenced the debate on women in track and field. For example, the fact that many working-class women and Black women participated in the sport in the United States contributed to the belief that the sport was inappropriate for upper-class white women. Sport administrators discouraged white women from engaging in track and field, fearing they would become "masculine." In the United States, Black women filled the void and started to dominate track and field. However, they also continued to experience gender prejudices and racial discrimination. US athletes Tidye Pickett and Louise Stokes earned spots on the 1932 US Olympic team, but were removed from the 4x100m relay team at the last minute and replaced with two white athletes who had not qualified for Olympics. During a time of significant anti-Black racism in the United States, officials did not consider Pickett and Stokes representatives of the country, despite their undisputed athletic abilities.[25] Four years later, Stokes was again demoted to the substitute runner in the relay team, but Pickett became the first African-American woman to compete in the Olympics in the 80m hurdles event and was the only Black woman on the relay team.[26]

In contrast to strength, endurance, or other exercises considered masculine, activities that highlighted femininity were much more tolerated amongst the white upper class. Not surprisingly, women's figure skating was the only event open to women at the Winter Olympics, which started in 1924 in Chamonix, France. The Norwegian skater Sonja Henie, who had already participated in Chamonix as an eleven-year-old, dominated the competitions in 1928 (St. Moritz, Switzerland), 1932 (Lake Placid, United States), and 1936 (Garmisch-Partenkirchen, Germany), winning three successive Olympic titles. While extremely talented, Henie added feminine charms, short skirts, and dancing choreographies to her performances, which judges and audiences alike perceived favorably. Her impact also transformed the sport of figure skating from a relatively gender-neutral sport to a feminine activity, later considered unsuitable for men.[27] Henie later became a movie star in Hollywood.

The celebration of Henie stood in stark contrast to the skepticism received by the few women competing in the sport of track and field. Journalists regularly criticized the appearance of Babe Didrikson, the 1932 Olympic gold medal winner mentioned above. Didrikson's blatant disregard of conventional gender norms added fuel to the fire for those who feared track and field produced mannish women.[28]

Sonja Henie at the 1936 Winter Olympic Games in Garmisch-Partenkirchen, Germany. Wikimedia Commons.

Two other early stars of women's track and field received similar criticism. Throughout the mid-1930s, sprinters Helen Stephens (United States) and Stella Walsh (Poland) dominated the 100m. Born to Missouri farmers, Stephens had developed strength through the daily operations of the farm, which allowed her to disregard contemporary gender restrictions. Walsh, who came from a working-class family and became the first woman to run the 100m in less than twelve seconds, was speedy and muscular. Both received criticism for their appearances throughout their careers by those concerned about the supposed masculinizing effects of track and field.

Some even questioned the two athletes' sex and accused them of being male imposters. These concerns culminated at the 1936 Berlin Olympic Games, during which Stephens won the gold medal ahead of Walsh, who took silver. Immediately after the race, Polish press reports claimed Stephens was a man. Stephens responded that she had been sex-tested before competition by the American Olympic Committee (AOC), suggesting sport officials were also concerned about the appearances of (their own) female competitors.[29] Walsh said medical doctors also inspected her ahead of many events, and she regularly passed the examinations.

Sport organizations found further support for their skepticism in the case of a German high jumper, who finished fourth in the women's event. This competitor later identified as a man, Heinrich Ratjen. Though some people speculated that the German Nazi regime had forced Ratjen to fraudulently participate as a woman, police records and medical reports prove this accusation was false. Ratjen was identified female at birth, despite having ambiguities in anatomy, and raised as a girl. In 1938, the German civil registry officially changed Ratjen's sex from female to male. Ratjen was exonerated of all charges but forced to return his medals. Even though he was not a male masquerader, Ratjen's case was later used by the IAAF and IOC as an example of a male imposter in women's sport.[30]

One of the most outspoken sport leaders against gender nonconforming women was US administrator Avery Brundage. Brundage, who would later serve as IOC President from 1952 until 1972, first served as the AOC President in Berlin. While in Germany, he grew anxious about the participation of muscular women. "I am fed up to the ears with women as track and field competitors," he explained after the Games. Their "charms sink to less than zero. . . . (and) they are ineffective and unpleasing on the track." He later advocated for sex tests for female competitors, "to make sure they were really 100% female." The IOC decided to pass this request to the international sport federations, with the

IAAF becoming the first federation to implement mandatory sex testing after the Second World War.[31]

In summary, the inclusion of women's track and field into the Olympic programme sparked concerns about Olympians' femininity. Many competitors did not conform to the traditional gender norms and the beauty ideals men foresaw for women. Race and class dynamics underpinned the concerns in some countries. The IAAF and IOC in particular grew worried about women who embodied strength and muscularity.

Global Contexts of Women's Sport

Even though competitive women's sport advanced significantly throughout the interwar period, participation at international events remained largely restricted to upper-class Western women. The amateur rule prevented most working-class women from competing. In addition, women's liberation movements gained less traction in other areas. As a result, most female Olympians initially hailed from European and North American countries. However, women in other parts of the world increasingly competed in organized sport, paving the way for their future participation in the Olympics.

The Olympic Movement reached a new pinnacle in international attention at the 1936 Berlin Olympics. A record 3,632 men and 331 women from 49 nations participated. German organizers erected a new Olympic Stadium that held 110,000 spectators and the Games were televised for the first time to a national audience. Organizers achieved these superlatives for political reasons. When the Nazi Party, officially named the National Socialist German Workers' Party (NSDAP), came to power in 1933, leaders considered the Games, which had been awarded to Berlin previously at the 29th IOC Session in 1931, as an opportunity to promote their ideals of racial supremacy and antisemitism.

The National Socialists applied the principle of cooptation to all facets of the German political and societal systems. In the new totalitarian state, based on racist ideologies, no other political or societal powers outside the Nazi Party were supposed to exist. The Nazis demanded that existing institutions and organizations disband or integrate into the NSDAP. Rejection led to compulsory liquidation. This "Nazification" strategy also infiltrated sport. According to the NSDAP, all forms of physical exercise served to benefit the regime and strengthen the Aryan race. The NSDAP systematically dismantled sport clubs and organizations with different political ideologies, such as worker's sport or Jewish sport clubs.

German fencer Helene Mayer (right) giving the "Nazi Salute" at the 1936 Berlin Olympics. Wikimedia Commons.

National Socialists encouraged physical activities for men, but largely discouraged women's participation. They agreed that women should not participate in "excessive" competitive sport, but instead remain restricted to their "maternal destiny."[32] The 1936 Berlin Olympics was an exception, however. The leading National Socialists considered the propaganda goals of the event more important than the ideological role foreseen for women. Recognizing the lack of competition in most women's sports in other countries, they promoted women's national elite sport in preparation for the Games. This strategy proved highly successful. German women won thirteen of forty-five medals in the women's events at the 1936 Games. Seven of the medals came from women's track and field.

Similar trends existed in Italy between 1922 until 1943, when Benito Mussolini led the Fascist regime. As in Nazi Germany, male athleticism and physical strength were key elements of Fascist body culture. Women therefore participated little in competitive sports. For example, at the 1932 Los Angeles Olympics, Italy performed impressively due to the nation's emphasis on sport, finishing second in the medal count behind the United States. However, no Italian woman participated at the Games.[33]

Likewise, Russian women initially had few opportunities in sport. In fact, before the Russian Revolution in 1917 when the Bolsheviks seized power, women had very little rights at all. Sport historian James Riordan argues that "women in all social classes were essentially slaves of their husbands."[34] Therefore, with few exceptions, women did not participate in sport. However, the Bolshevik Revolution, which abolished the monarchy and established socialism, led to a liberation of women. Leaders embraced principles of gender equality in early legislation. The socialist leaders also encouraged sport participation for both men and women, albeit not in a competitive way. Bolshevik leaders rejected the "Bourgeoisie" Olympics as a forum for capitalistic sports. After competing in the 1912 Olympics, Russia did not participate in the Games again until 1952, as the Soviet Union.

The Russians instead organized socialist mass sport events during the interwar era. Women participated in great numbers. For example, the International Workers' Olympiads, staged by the Socialist Workers' Sport International, occurred in 1925 (Frankfurt, Germany), 1931 (Vienna, Austria), and 1937 (Antwerp, Belgium). Female athletes competed in track and field starting in 1925, three years before they did in the Olympics.

Outside Europe and North America, Japan had the largest female contingency at the Olympic Games in the interwar years. After sending an all-male Olympic team in 1912—the first Asian country to do so—Japanese women competed at the 1928, 1932, and 1936 Olympic Games and won several medals. The country had undergone a social transformation in the early twentieth century and invested in sport development for both men and women.[35] China sent its first female participant, sprinter Li Sen, to the 1936 Olympic Games. In South Asia, India participated in the Olympic Games from 1920 onwards, and their first delegation included female tennis player Nora Polley. It is of note that Polley was born in Great Britain and married a military officer in the Indian Army. The colonial sport structure significantly limited opportunities for Indian women.

Competitive sport reached the Middle East through French and British colonization in the early twentieth century. Some sport clubs permitted upper-class women to engage in physical activities, in line with the gender norms prevalent in the colonizing nations. Religious concerns also added obstacles, with interpretations of Islam varying between moderate participation for women and complete rejection.[36] No woman from the Middle East participated in the Olympics prior to the First World War. In 1936, fencers Halet Çambel and Suat Fetgeri Aşani were the first Turkish women to compete at the Olympics.

Misao Yokota of Japan in the 100m backstroke at the 1932 Los Angeles Olympics. Wikimedia Commons.

Maria Emma Hulga Lenk.
Photo: 100 Years Brazil Olympic Committee 1914-2014.

Similarly, when competitive sport spread to Latin America, women were mostly excluded from this process. The first woman from Latin America to participate in the Olympic Games was the Brazilian swimmer Maria Emma Hulda Lenk, who competed in the breaststroke at the 1932 Los Angeles Games. Her participation followed initiatives by Brazilian women in the early 1930s who organized national championships for women and established their own clubs.[37] Mexico also sent its first female Olympian, javelin thrower María Uribe, that year. Other Latin American women followed in 1936 when Raquel Martinez (Chile) and Jeannette Campbell (Argentina) participated in the swimming competition with Lenk.

Research on African women's participation in competitive sport prior to the Second World War is scarce. Barbara Nash, a white South African woman, was the first female Olympian from the continent. She competed in swimming at the 1920 Olympics. White South African and Rhodesian women participated at the 1934 Women's World Games in London, largely due to their nations' colonial ties. Black African athletes from other African countries under European control were not permitted to compete at international sport events until the period of decolonialization after the Second World War (see chapter 3).

Finally, in Australia and New Zealand, women's sport participation followed the same path as in Great Britain. Some upper-class women contended in sport in the late nineteenth century, but social restrictions applied. For example, ordinances segregated public swimming pools by sex and men could not watch women's swimming. However, when swimming was added to the Olympic program in 1912, two Australian women competed, despite resistance from their national sport organization. With public support, Fanny Durack and Wilhelmina Wylie managed to swim at the events in Stockholm, finishing first and second, respectively, in the 100m freestyle. During the 1920s and 1930s, women from Australia and New Zealand continued to appear at the Olympic Games in small numbers.

Conclusion

The World Wars ushered in significant changes for women in the Olympics. First, the absence of men due to military duties during the First World War required middle- and upper-class white women in Europe and North America to join the labor force. As a result, white women began to engage in physical activities more frequently. The first women's sport competitions, clubs, and leagues emerged in the late 1910s. Second, during the interwar period, debates in the Olympic Movement centered on the inclusion of women's track and field. The efforts of French feminist Alice Milliat to organize independent international sport competitions for women pressured the IOC to include the sport at the 1928 Amsterdam Olympics. The number of women participating in the Games therefore increased steadily throughout the 1920s and 1930s. The 1936 Berlin Olympics saw the highest participation of female competitors with 331. Yet, while Milliat aimed to maintain a separate women's sport movement, her efforts were short-lived. The male Olympic sport administrators integrated women's sport into their male-dominated sport organizations as a way to maintain control over all governance decisions. Finally, female participants at the Olympics in the interwar era primarily came from Asia, Europe, North America, and nations with colonial ties to Great Britain and France. Only very few women of color participated in the Olympic Games during this period.

In many ways, the concerns about women's physical appearances that started with their introduction in track and field heightened over the next few decades. The Second World War forced the IOC to cancel the Games planned for Tokyo in 1940 and London in 1944. When international sport resumed after the war, sport leaders faced a new global climate. Countries had divided into east versus west. The Olympics gained new importance as a result and the question about women's proper place in the movement surfaced yet again.

> ### Discussion Questions
>
> - What were the obstacles to women's participation at the Olympics during the interwar era?
>
> - How did men justify excluding women from their sports and sports organizations? How were these justifications shaped by race, class, and gender norms?
>
> - How did Alice Milliat lose control over the women's sport movement after the 1930s? What were the advantages and disadvantages of seeking to integrate women's sport competitions into the Olympics?
>
> - Would women athletes, in the past and present, be better served by separate, women-run sport organizations? Why or why not?

CHAPTER 3

Women in the Cold War Olympics

Women's Olympic Milestones, 1948-1980

77 women (592 men) compete at the St. Moritz Winter Olympics. Women compete in the downhill and slalom for the first time. Swiss skier Hedy Schlunegger wins the first women's gold medal in the downhill and US skier Gretchen Fraser wins the first women's gold in the slalom.

1948 390 women (3,714 men) compete at the London Summer Olympics. Women from Bermuda, Iceland, Jamaica, and the Republic of Korea participate for the first time.

US high jumper Alice Coachman is the first Black-American woman to win a gold medal at the London Games.

1952 109 women (585 men) compete at the Oslo Winter Olympics.

Women's Olympic Milestones, 1948-1980, continued...

1952

519 women (4,436 men) compete at the Helsinki Summer Olympics. Women from Bulgaria, Hong Kong, Israel, Portugal, Saarland, Singapore, the Soviet Union, Uruguay, and Venezuela participate for the first time.

The Soviet Union returns to the Helsinki Olympics. The country wins seventy-one medals, twenty-three of which are earned by women. Soviet discus thrower Nina Romashkova is the first Soviet athlete to win a gold medal.

1956

134 women (687 men) compete at the Cortina d'Ampezzo Winter Olympics.

376 women (2,938 men) compete at the Melbourne Summer Olympics. Women from Cuba, Guyana, Indonesia, Kenya, Malaya, and the Philippines participate for the first time.

Swimmer Margaret Northrop is the first woman from Kenya at the Olympics. She is the first African woman, not from South Africa, to compete.

Australian runner Betty Cuthbert wins three gold medals in track and field at the 1956 Melbourne Olympics.

Women's Olympic Milestones, 1948-1980, continued...

144 women (521 men) compete at the Squaw Valley Winter Olympics. Women participate in speed skating for the first time. Skater Helga Haase of the United Team of Germany wins the first women's gold in the 500m.

1960 611 women (5,338 men) compete at the Rome Olympics. Women from Panama, Puerto Rico, Rhodesia, and Taiwan (later as Chinese Taipei) participate for the first time.

Sprinter Wilma Rudolph is the first US woman to win three gold medals at a single Olympics.

199 women (892 men) compete at the 1964 Innsbruck Winter Olympics.

Cross-country skier Dorjgotovyn Pürevloov is the first woman from Mongolia, and speed skater Han Pil-Hwa is the first woman from the Democratic People's Republic of Korea, to compete at the Olympics.

1964

678 women (5,151 men) compete at the Tokyo Summer Olympics. Women from Ghana, Iran, Malaysia, Nigeria, Peru, Thailand, Uganda, Zambia, and Zimbabwe participate for the first time.

Women compete in volleyball for the first time. The Japanese team wins the first gold medal in the sport.

Women's Olympic Milestones, 1948-1980, continued...

	211 women (947 men) compete at the 1968 Grenoble Winter Olympics.
	Alpine skier Marta Bühler is the first woman from Liechtenstein at the Olympics.
	781 women (5,516 men) compete at the Mexico City Summer Olympics. Women from Colombia, Costa Rica, Curaçao/Netherlands Antilles, East Germany, Ecuador, El Salvador, South Vietnam, and West Germany participate for the first time.
1968	The International Olympic Committee introduces mandatory doping controls and sex tests.
	Mexican sprinter Enriqueta Basilio is the first woman to light the Olympic cauldron
	The high altitude of Mexico City helps several track and field athletes set records. Wyomia Tyus of the United States (100m), Irena Szewińska of Poland (200m), Viorica Viscopoleanu of Romania (long jump), Margitta Gummel of East Germany (shot put), and the US 4 x 100m relay team set world records. Madeline Madding of the United States (800m) and Maureen Caird of Australia (80m hurdles) set Olympic records.
1972	205 women (801 men) compete at the Sapporo Winter Olympics.

Women's Olympic Milestones, 1948-1980, continued...

1972

1,059 women (6,075 men) compete at the Munich Summer Olympics. Women from Albania, the Bahamas, Barbados, Cambodia, Haiti, Lebanon, Malawi, Morocco, Nicaragua, the Syrian Arab Republic, and Trinidad and Tobago participate for the first time.

Soviet gymnast Olga Korbut is a fan favorite at the 1972 Summer Olympics. The "Sparrow from Minsk" wins three gold medals and one silver.

Women compete in archery for the first time since 1920. US archer Doreen Wilber wins the gold medal in the women's individual event.

231 women (892 men) compete at the Innsbruck Winter Olympics.

1976

1,260 women (4,824 men) compete at the Montreal Summer Olympics. Women from the Ivory Coast (Côte d'Ivoire), Dominican Republic, Fiji, San Marino, Senegal, Tunisia, and the United States Virgin Islands participate for the first time.

Romanian gymnast Nadia Comaneci is the first gymnast to earn a 10.0 on the uneven bars.

Soviet runner Tatyana Kazankina wins gold medals in the 800m and 1500m.

Women's Olympic Milestones, 1948-1980, continued...

1980

232 women (840 men) compete at the Lake Placid Winter Olympics. Alpine skier Lina Aristodimou is the first woman from Cyprus at the Olympics.

1,115 women (4,064 men) compete at the Moscow Summer Olympics. Women from Angola, Benin, Cameroon, Congo, Ethiopia, Lao People's Democratic Republic, Libya, Madagascar, Mali, Malta, Mozambique, Seychelles, Sierra Leone, the United Republic of Tanzania, and Vietnam participate for the first time.

65 countries, including the United States, boycott the Moscow Olympics.

Historians call the time following the Second World War the Cold War. During this period, from mid-century to the early 1990s, the world split along geopolitical lines. Nations divided into "East" versus "West" in geography, ideology, influence, and politics. Because each side attempted to demonstrate superiority over the other, the Olympics became a particularly powerful forum to display strength to an international audience. Though Eastern and Western Bloc countries agreed on the importance of international events as a way to show power, they disagreed about women's role in that process. Led by the Soviet Union, Eastern Bloc nations more readily approved of women's participation in sport. In contrast, Western Bloc countries were less likely to encourage rigorous, physical training and involvement in events considered masculine. As a result, throughout the Cold War, Eastern Bloc women dominated more taxing Olympic sports, such as gymnastics, Nordic skiing, and track and field. Western Bloc women dominated Olympic sports considered more appropriately feminine, such as alpine skiing, diving, and swimming.

This chapter examines women in the Cold War Olympics. The prowess of Czechoslovakian, East German, Polish, Romanian, and Soviet women helped Eastern nations win Olympic medals and gain international attention. However, their successes also led to accusations that the women were either using performance enhancing substances or were male imposters. As a result, the International Olympic Committee (IOC) introduced doping tests and sex checks. Women Olympians during the Cold War Games helped generate a tempered acceptance of women's sport, one which was undermined by fears about athletes who looked too strong, too powerful, and too muscular.

East versus West

Geopolitical divisions after the Second World War sparked the Cold War, separating the world into "East" versus "West." It is important to note that the notion of the "East" and "West" has had various meanings and locations in different historical moments. For this chapter, "East" refers to Eastern Bloc countries in Central and Eastern Europe, as well as in Eastern and Southeastern Asia. The Eastern Bloc was predominantly communist and under the influence of the Soviet Union (USSR). "West" in this chapter refers to Western Block countries in Western Europe and North America. The Western Bloc was predominantly capitalist, led by the United States (USA).

Direct military confrontations did not occur between the "superpowers," the Soviet Union and United States. However, Eastern Bloc and Western Bloc countries instead engaged in cultural confrontations to display their dominance. This struggle for soft power extended into the realm of sport. Throughout the Cold War, international competitions gained significance as Eastern and Western nations saw them as opportunities to demonstrate superiority. As historians Robert Edelman and Christopher Young explain, "more states than ever craved symbolic capital through athletic endeavor."[1] Cold War concerns thus increased dramatically when the Soviet Union returned to the Olympics in 1952.

Soviet athletes did not participate in the 1948 London Games, which allowed Olympic leaders to avoid Cold War tensions. Geopolitical hostilities influenced the Olympics in a different way, as the London organizers did not invite Germany or Japan to attend, due to their role in the Second World War. The war further affected the Games as they occurred in a war-ravaged city and a financially-strapped country. Called the "Austerity Games," London had little time to prepare and almost had to forgo hosting due to economic problems. Despite these difficulties, 390 women (compared to 4,104 men) competed in athletics, canoeing, diving, fencing, gymnastics, shooting, and swimming. Women's track and field expanded to ten events—with the addition of the 200m, long jump, and shot put. The expansion helped foster several important milestones. US high jumper Alice Coachman became the first Black woman from the United States to win an Olympic gold medal. Dutch runner Fanny Blankers-Koen, nicknamed "the Flying Housewife," became an international celebrity for winning four gold medals in track and field: in the 100m, 200m, 80m hurdles, and 4x100m relay. Blankers-Koen, who upheld conventional notions of femininity, received international adoration and fandom, while Coachman's accomplishment received little attention within the white US presses.

London 1948 Olympic Games, Athletics, high jump Women - Alice Coachman (USA) 1st. Courtesy of the International Olympic Committee.

The Soviet Union rejoined the Olympic Movement in 1952. During the "Cold War Olympics," Eastern and Western nations faced off and attached increased geopolitical importance to the Games. As people looked to the Olympics as a way to demonstrate superiority, they divided on the acceptability of women's involvement. Whereas Eastern leaders encouraged women to participate in a variety of activities, including those considered masculine, women in Western countries were restrained by widespread beliefs about acceptable femininity. The different ideals influenced the sports women played and the numbers of medals they won during the Cold War Games.

Women's Olympic Sport in the East

Eastern and Western societies had different ideas about the role of women at the Olympics. Leaders in Eastern Bloc countries more favorably viewed women's participation, particularly in the Soviet Union and East Germany, for four overlapping reasons. First, Eastern officials believed physical activity was an important way to develop the communist workforce.[2] Labor was a central component of everyday life, which leaders believed could be enhanced through one's participation in physical activity. Women were therefore encouraged to participate at the same levels as men. For example, East German state leaders viewed physical activity as a way to mold men and women into the socialist way of life.[3] Likewise, the Soviet Union encouraged mass participation for everyone.[4] This arrangement allowed for greater gender equality in physical contests, though inequalities did not completely disappear.[5] Soviet sport leaders did not consider certain activities, such as boxing and wrestling, appropriate for women.[6]

Second, many communist countries created expansive sport structures that trained both male and female athletes. The government organized, funded, and controlled these programs. Pioneered by the Soviet Union, such sport systems included centralized training regiments aimed at improving international performances in all sports. Men and women alike participated in and benefited from the setup. For example, East German leaders introduced a three-rung, pyramid-style setup for children that included Training Centres for mass participation, Children and Youth Sport Schools for select individuals, and Sport Clubs for elite athletes. In 1989, over 67,000 young athletes participated in Training Centres, over 9,000 in Sports Schools, and over 3,000 in Sports Clubs.[7] Romanian sport leaders organized a similar system for athletes, which involved identifying talented boys and girls at young ages and centralizing their training in selective schools.[8] The elite "Romanian School of Gymnastics" produced world-renowned gymnasts, including Nadia Comăneci, the first Romanian gymnast to win the Olympic all-around title in 1976.

Third, Eastern Bloc countries viewed success in sport as an indication of international power and saw women's victories as necessary to achieve this goal. "Women played a significant role in establishing the reputation of eastern bloc countries as the world's most competitive sporting nations," explains sport historian Amanda Schweinbenz."[9] Supporting women in the Olympics achieved two aims. It increased the total number of medals won in international competitions. This was clearly shown in the USA-USSR Track and Field Dual Meet Series, contests that pitted the superpowers against each other from 1958-1985. During the nineteen meetings, the Soviet Union claimed fifteen victories and one tie, largely due to the points earned by Soviet women. The US women only topped the Soviet women once in 1969, 70-67. Seven years later, the USSR women outscored the US women, 104-42. Second, supporting women's sport also offered an example of gender equality to a global audience.

Eastern Bloc leaders argued that communist countries treated women better than capitalist countries, as indicated by their sport participation. According to scholars Mike Dennis and Jonathan Grix, East German sport leaders recognized that the "rich haul of medals" earned by its women provided "further evidence of the emancipation of women in the GDR and of the progressive nature of socialism."[10] In contrast to women's sport in the West, officials argued, women's sport in the East received greater support.

Fourth, to increase the numbers of medals won by women, Eastern leaders encouraged women to train rigorously for the Olympics. For example, as Dennis and Grix write, East German leaders "devised training programmes whose intensity and heavy load were regarded in many countries as incompatible with traditional notions of femininity."[11] British diver Elizabeth Ferris echoed this sentiment and remembered that Eastern European women "were much more willing to train very hard" than their Western counterparts, resulting in significant medal hauls.[12] Taken together, the importance of physical labor, development of athletic training centers, support for women's sport, and strenuous training regiments allowed Eastern European women to excel at the Olympics.

Women's Olympic Sport in the West

The reception to women athletes in Western countries was more tempered. First, as noted in previous chapters, Western medical guidelines suggested strenuous physically activity was inappropriate—and possibly dangerous—for white, middle-class women.[13] Though women had challenged this idea for decades, the belief persisted and restricted women's athletic opportunities. For example, medical authorities warned that women's lighter bone structures and less-muscular physiques made them physiologically unfit to run for prolonged amounts of time. Some practitioners even suggested doing so would harm their reproductive organs. This led sport officials to ban women from distance events. Western track and field leaders cited medical beliefs about harm when prohibiting women from the marathon throughout the 1950s and 1960s.[14]

Second, based on these medical ideas about harm, Western sport leaders continued to support modified versions of competitions for women. These activities aimed to maintain women's health, femininity, and grace. Writing in 1965, US physical educator Eleanor Metheny described "wholly appropriate" sports for white women as those that: created aesthetically pleasing patterns, such as figure skating; required a light object or light implement, such as croquet; or had a spatial barrier that prevented bodily contact, such as tennis. She depicted "not appropriate" sports as those where: an opponent is overcome by bodily contact, such as boxing; a heavy object is overcome by bodily force, such as the shot put; or the body is projected over long distances, such as the marathon.[15] These ideas were apparent in many Western nations. For example, in Italy women were encouraged to participate in activities that were "less fatiguing and violent than men's sport," such as archery, golf, gymnastics, and swimming.[16] Similarly, when sport leaders in Canada facilitated women's participation, they did so "in a way that did not contest restrictive patriarchal views on female abilities."[17] Western social norms interpreted muscularity and strength as at odds with femininity.

Third, Western audiences disparaged the successes of Eastern Bloc women by mocking their appearances. Capitalist countries suggested communism harmed women's natural femininity and described Eastern Bloc women as "graceless, shapeless and sexless."[18] For example, *New York Times* reporter Arthur Daley complained that Soviet track and field athlete Tamara Press was "big enough to play tackle for the Chicago Bears," while her sister Irina Press was "about the size of a running guard."[19] US Olympian Jan Romary similarly described the East German women as "very masculine-looking" and suggested some of whom "you wouldn't want to meet in a dark ally."[20] Insulting Eastern Bloc women's looks further discouraged Western women's involvement in physically taxing sports that required muscularity; they were instead encouraged to "remain attractive, feminine, and above all not give any appearance of masculinity."[21]

US 4x100m relay runners Wilma Rudolph, Lucinda Williams, Barbara Jones, and Martha Hudson at the 1960 Rome Olympics. Wikimedia Commons.

However, not all women experienced the hostility to their participation in the same way. Not as burdened by the restrictions of white femininity, Black women excelled in certain sports, specifically track and field. As historian Susan K. Cahn argues, "black women stepped into an arena largely abandoned by middle-class white women . . . and began to blaze a remarkable trail of national and international excellence."[22] As noted above, high jumper Alice Coachman was the first Black woman to win a gold medal in 1948. Sprinter Wilma Rudolph became the first US woman to win three gold medals at a single Olympics in 1960. When the United States earned three Olympic track and field medals in 1956 (Soviet women earned eight), they all stemmed from the achievements of Black women.[23] However, their successes also reinforced stereotypes of Black women as less feminine than white women.[24]

These different expectations of gender in the East and West resulted in varying levels of success at the Olympic Games.

Women's Olympic Sport in Africa

Although the United States and the Soviet Union dominated Cold War headlines, Eastern versus Western tensions touched all corners of the globe. Cold War confrontations extended into the "periphery," a term used by historians to describe areas outside of North America and Europe that were significantly impacted by the conflict.[25] Direct military clashes occurred—for example, the Korean and Vietnam wars—as did imperialistic efforts to align governments to capitalism or communism. Such struggles played out in Africa and South America, with different effects on women's elite sport.

European countries remained in control of most of Africa during the interwar era. By 1945, only four African countries had gained independence: Egypt, Ethiopia, Liberia, and South Africa, though lingering effects of colonialism remained intact. Growing independence movements, coupled with Cold War dynamics, led to decolonization throughout the mid-twentieth century. African leaders across the continent fought for autonomy against colonial rule. The two superpowers supported such efforts in order to keep the other nation from gaining control—however, neither the Soviet ideal of communism nor the US ideal of democracy fully emerged. From 1945 to the end of 1960, over twenty African countries achieved autonomy. With sovereignty, they formed National Olympic Committees (NOCs) and joined the Olympic Movement. South African men and Egyptian men first participated in 1904 and 1920, respectively; South African women and Egyptian women first participated in 1920 and 1984[26], respectively. However, when most African NOCs first contended during the Cold War, they did so with teams entirely composed of men. Table 3.1 shows the time difference between African countries' NOC's debuts and their inclusion of women at the Olympics.

Table 3.1: African NOCs' Summer Olympic Debuts, 1952-1968, and Their Inclusion of Women

National Olympic Committee	Year of First Olympic Participation	Year of First Female Olympic Participation	Difference
Ghana / Gold Coast	1952	1964	12
Nigeria	1952	1964	12
Ethiopia	1956	1980	24
Kenya	1956	1956	0
Liberia	1956	1984	28
Uganda	1956	1964	8
Morocco	1960	1972	12
Sudan	1960	2000	40
Tunisia	1960	1976	16
Algeria	1964	1988	24
Cameroon	1964	1980	16
Chad	1964	1992	28

Congo	1964	1980	16
Ivory Coast / Côte d'Ivoire	1964	1976	12
Madagascar	1964	1980	16
Mali	1964	1980	16
Niger	1964	1996	32
Senegal	1964	1976	12
United Republic of Tanzania / Tanganyika	1964	1980	16
Zambia / Northern Rhodesia	1964	1964	0
Central African Republic	1968	1992	24
Democratic Republic of the Congo / Zaire	1968	1984	16
Guinea	1968	1992	24
Libya	1968	1980	12
Sierra Leone	1968	1980	12

Similar to the restrictions women experienced elsewhere, gender norms limited African women's participation in the Olympics. Colonialism, racism, and religion further hindered their inclusion into elite sport. Although beliefs and practices varied by location, in general, competitive sport in Africa was an activity reserved for men during both the colonial and post-colonial eras. For example, Nigerian leaders regraded women "as the weaker sex" and worried that their "natural charm, beauty, and femininity may be destroyed by participation in vigorous physical activities."[27] Colonial ideology about female frailty, including concerns about the harms physical activity caused women's reproductive organs, reinforced these ideas.[28]

Colonialism also created obstacles for African women. Until 1956, the only African women who competed at the Olympics did so for South Africa. The country's system of apartheid—institutionalized racial segregation and oppression that allowed the minority white population to dominate economically, politically, and socially—allowed the South African NOC to only send white athletes to the Games. White-controlled national governing bodies refused to allow non-white athletes to participate, thereby blocking their access to international, elite sport, including the Olympics.[29] As a result, Black women in South Africa faced restrictions due to both their gender and race. After ignoring the pleas from Black athletes for years, the IOC voted in 1963 to suspend South Africa for its racial discrimination. South Africa did not compete in the Olympics again until the 1992 Barcelona Olympics.[30] The country's first racially diverse team included eleven non-white athletes on its ninety-seven-member team.

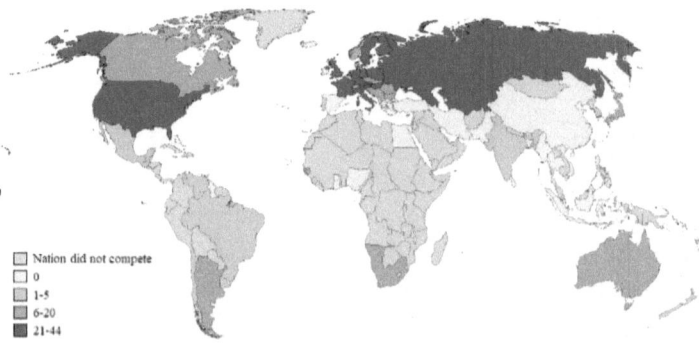

Figure 3.1 The Number of Women Who Competed per Country at the 1952 Summer Olympics[31]

African women nevertheless chipped away at the intersecting obstacles of colonialism, racism, and sexism to compete at the Olympics. In 1956, Kenyan swimmer Margaret Northrop swam in the 100m freestyle event, becoming the first African woman from outside of South Africa to compete at the Games. Four years later, Rhodesia (later renamed Zimbabwe) included five women on its Olympic team; they competed in diving and swimming events. During the 1964 Tokyo Games, four additional African NOCs included female Olympians: Ghana, Nigeria, Uganda, and Zambia. Figure 3.1 illustrates the number of women who competed by country at the 1952 Olympics.

These international tensions and domestic hurdles meant that European and North American women continued to dominate national teams and the Olympic podium. With some exceptions, the Olympic teams with the highest percentage of female Olympians were from Europe. When Eastern Bloc female Olympians started to surpass Western Bloc female Olympians, the IOC introduced new policies to ensure the authenticity of their victories.

Women's Olympic Performances during the Cold War

Beliefs about appropriate femininity created different levels of success at the Olympics. Due to the support they received at home, Eastern European women dominated many competitions during the Cold War Olympics. At the 1952 Helsinki Summer Olympics, 519 women competed in eight sports. Organizers invited Japanese and German athletes; however, following the Second World War, Germany divided into the Federal Republic of Germany (West Germany) and the German Democratic Republic (East Germany). A United Team of Germany, comprised of East and West Germans, competed at the 1956, 1960, and 1964 Olympics. From 1968-1988, East Germany and West Germany participated as separate NOCs. The IOC introduced six new gymnastics disciplines for women in Helsinki: the balance beam, floor exercise, individual-all around; team portable apparatus; uneven bars; and vault. Eastern European gymnasts excelled in the new disciplines, earning all fifteen of the individual available medals. They also swept the podium in the team all-around and claimed silver and bronze in the team-portable apparatus event. Soviet women helped the country finish second in the medal count, only five behind the United States. They earned twenty-three of the country's seventy-one medals that year; US women earned eight. Hungary finished third in the 1952 medal count with forty-two medals, sixteen of which came from its women. This trend continued throughout the Cold War. Table 3.2 shows the percent of medals women won for the countries that finished in the top four of the medal count at the 1976 Summer Olympics.

Table 3.2: Percent of Medals Won by Women in Top Four Countries of 1976 Summer Olympic Medal Count

	Country	Percent of Medals Won by Women
1	Soviet Union	28.80%
2	United States	18.10%
3	East Germany	53.30%
4	West Germany	15.40%

Along with differences in the total number of medals earned, Eastern and Western Olympians also excelled in different sports. Eastern European women tended to shine in physically taxing disciplines, such as track and field and Nordic skiing. White, Western European women tended to find success in disciplines considered more refined and graceful, such as alpine skiing and diving. For example, during the 1960 Winter and Summer Olympics, Soviet women claimed the top four finishes in the 10km cross-country ski race, finished second in the 3x5km cross-country relay, and earned eight medals in track and field, six of which came from field events. They did not medal in alpine skiing or diving. In contrast, US skiers claimed one-third of the medals in alpine skiing and diving during the same Games, and did not earn a place on the podium in cross-country skiing. The four medals US women won in track and field all came from the efforts of Black women. This included the three gold medals won by runner Wilma Rudolph. Similarly, at the 1964 Tokyo Olympics, Czechoslovakian, East German, Hungarian, and Soviet women earned all the individual medals available in women's gymnastics.[32] The sport had not evolved into an acrobatic discipline with younger athletes; at the time it was considered a more masculine pursuit. Soviet gymnast Larisa Latynina won two gold, two silver, and two bronze medals in 1964. This brought her total medal count to eighteen, making her the most decorated Olympian at the time.

Bronze medalist Larisa Latynina of the Soviet Union on the podium during the uneven bars medal ceremony of the women's artistic gymnastics during the 1964 Summer Olympics. Wikimedia Commons.

Likewise, at the 1976 Winter and Summer Olympics, West German women won three of nine possible medals in alpine skiing, five in track and field, and zero in cross-country skiing; East German women earned zero medals in alpine skiing, nineteen in track and field, and the bronze in the 4-5km cross-country relay. Table 3.3 and 3.4 illustrate the different areas of expertise by showing the number of available individual medals (i.e., excluding relays) won by US and USSR women in events considered graceful (alpine skiing and diving) and events considered grueling (track and field and cross-country skiing). Western women excelled in competitions like alpine skiing and diving; Eastern women excelled in competitions like cross-country skiing and track and field.

Table 3.3 Number of Individual Available Medals Won by US and USSR Women in Select Winter Events, 1952-1976

	Alpine Skiing			Cross-Country Skiing		
Olympics	US	USSR	Medals Available	US	USSR	Medals Available
1952	2	DNC	9	0	DNC	3
1956	0	0	9	0	2	3
1960	3	0	9	0	3	3
1964	2	0	9	0	5	6
1968	0	0	9	0	2	6
1972	2	0	9	0	2	6

Table 3.4 Number of Individual Available Medals Won by US and USSR Women in Select Summer Events, 1952-1976.

	Diving			Track and Field		
Olympics	US	USSR	Medals Available	US	USSR	Medals Available
1952	5	0	6	0	10	24
1956	5	0	6	2	8	24
1960	2	1	6	3	8	27
1964	3	1	6	3	8	33
1968	3	2	6	3	5	33
1972	1	0	6	2	4	36

The performances of Eastern Bloc women challenged Western ideas about appropriate femininity. For example, writing in *Olympic Games 1964*, the official publication on the Innsbruck Winter Olympics, Austro-Hungarian writer Harald Lechenperg discussed cross-country skiing and commented that "there is still divided opinion as to whether the strenuous [event] is good for the female sex" and added that many Western countries remained "revolted by this sport which is so taxing on the body." Lechenperg acknowledged that the Soviet Union was an exception as "both men and women were exposed to the same intensity of training."[33] These feelings of disdain stemmed from the muscular appearances and successful achievements of Eastern European women, which eventually led to the introduction of new testing policies at the Olympics.

The Introduction of Sex Controls and Dope Tests at the Olympics

Along with Western sport leaders, the IOC was also concerned about the strength, muscularity, and successes of the Eastern European women during the Cold War. They believed that Eastern countries used either male imposters or doped women to win medals. Rather than mirror the support for women's sport in Eastern Europe, they disliked "the challenge that increasing number of Cold War female Olympians presented to the dominant images of 'appropriate' gender appearance, demeanour, and performance."[34] Sport leaders responded by introducing mandatory sex control and anti-doping tests during the Cold War.

The International Association of Athletics (IAAF), the international federation that oversaw track and field, was the first to introduce sex tests into competition. It sporadically checked "suspicious" women—those who looked too muscular, ran too fast, or threw too far—in the 1930s and 1940s through physical exams. In 1966, the IAAF required all women undergo an anatomical investigation on-site prior to competition.[35] British athlete Mary Peters described the check as "the most crude and degrading experience I have ever known in my life."[36] Athlete dislike of the "nude parade" convinced the IAAF to embrace a new check in 1967, the Barr body test. The Barr body test, a relatively new scientific technique, used chromosomes to determine sex. Sport leaders embraced the Barr body test because they incorrectly believed people split neatly into XX and XY chromosomal makeups.[37] However, scientists immediately informed the federation that no single criteria could identify a person's sex, including chromosomes. The IAAF ignored the warning, introduced the Barr body test requirement at the 1967 European Cup, and barred Polish sprinter Ewa Kłobukowska for having a "mosaic" of chromosomes.[38] Although Kłobukowska was not a male imposter and had passed a visual inspection the previous year, the IAAF banned her from competition and erased her records.

IOC leaders used Kłobukowska's supposed failure to introduce sex testing into the Olympics. French doctor and later IOC Medical

Commission member Jacques Thiebault argued that, regarding the "so-called females who are as strong as oxen"—presumably a reference to Eastern European track and field athletes—"it is inevitable that sooner or later the real representatives of the weaker sex will feel persecuted and will demand their feminine records be attributed to them."[39] Based on such thoughts, the IOC implemented sex control in 1968 using the Barr body test. As scholars Rob Beamish and Ian Ritchie explain, "the attempt to control participants through sex testing was simultaneously an attempt to re-establish and reinforce the dominant Western image of femininity and female appropriate appearance and behaviour."[40] In other words, sex testing served to protect the "real representatives" from the "so-called females." Throughout the Cold War and beyond, from 1968 to 1999, the IOC mandated sex tests for all female Olympians.

Sport leaders also worried that Eastern Bloc women used performance-enhancing substances, specifically steroids. Fears in North America and Western Europe about steroid-use initially stemmed from rumors that Nazis soldiers had abused substances, then later morphed into accusations that Eastern Bloc countries used them to help achieve communist aims, including in sport.[41] For example, British newspaper accounts accused Soviet athletes of cheating through equipment manipulation, state-sponsored funding, and doping.[42] The IOC Medical Commission intervened by publishing the first prohibited substance list in 1967. Officials checked for alcohols, amphetamines, cannabis, cocaine, ephedrine, opiates, and vasodilators. The lack of an effective testing mechanism meant the IOC did not test for steroids until 1976.[43]

Steroid use was widespread among athletes in numerous sports, including those from Western countries. For example, at the 1976 US Olympic trials, twenty-three US athletes failed the drug test. Not a single one was punished.[44] However, what distinguished East Germany from other countries was the state-sponsored nature of steroid administration. East German leaders administered Oral-Turinabol, an androgenic-anabolic steroid, to male Olympic-potentials starting in 1966. Steroid use for elite East German athletes was a requirement, not a choice, by 1974. Many women later reported being forced to ingest pills.[45] East German athletes experienced serious health ailments due to systematic doping, including breast and testicular cancer, fertility issues, heart disease, and liver tumors.

Despite the prevalence of doping in several countries, Western leaders particularly disliked the use of steroids by women. Reports pointed out the masculinizing effects women supposedly experienced through the ingestion of steroids, which included the development of facial hair, deepening of the voice, and increased muscularity. Accounts further described the appearances of Eastern Bloc women in negative terms. For example, US Olympian Rod Strachan commented that the East German swimmers did not look feminine. "They're quite a bit bigger than most of the men on the American team," he said. "They could go out for [American] football," a sport that epitomizes masculinity in the United States[46] Western sport leaders condemned Eastern sport leaders for embracing illegal substances, without acknowledging their own culpability in such practices, which lead to increased testing.

Beliefs about appropriate femininity convinced the IOC Medical Commission to simultaneously implement sex tests and doping controls at the Grenoble Winter Olympics. As Beamish and Ritchie explain. "sport leaders sought to eliminate drugs and alleged female impersonation which, it was felt, would help return women's sport to its more 'natural' form."[47] Though sex verification and doping controls were separate tests with distinct aims, many people conflated the two as achieving a singular purpose: to eliminate unfeminine women from the Olympics.

The confusion about the aims of the tests underscores the significance of gender in both sex and anti-doping control. Fears of masculinized, steroid-ingesting women Olympians added support for testing.

New Olympic Successes, New Olympic Sports

While the successes of powerful Eastern Bloc women during the Cold War Olympics helped spur the onset of sex testing and anti-doping controls, they also forced Western countries to change its athletic programming. When the Soviet women helped the USSR defeat the United States in the medal count, tensions between the appropriateness of women in athletic competitions versus the need for US women to win more medals surfaced. As sport scholar Jaime Schultz writes, "the 1950s marked a time of intense debate about whether and how to invigorate American women's sport."[48] Western sport leaders slowly increased training opportunities and funding for women's sport.

In addition to expanding opportunities for women in the West, Eastern countries successfully helped grow the Olympic programme. When the Soviet Union returned to international competition in 1952, it almost immediately petitioned for more women's events. More events for women meant more medals for the Soviet Union. In the 1950s, Soviet sport leaders lobbied the IOC for the addition of basketball, rowing, speed skating, and volleyball for women, as well as additional distances in cross-country skiing.[49] In 1960, the Soviet representative Konstantin Andrianov proposed including women in basketball, canoeing, cycling, equestrian, handball, rowing, shooting, volleyball, and speedskating. The efforts slowly paid off. The IOC incrementally added sporting opportunities for women throughout the Cold War: speed skating in 1960, new cross-country distances in 1964, volleyball in 1972, and basketball, handball, and rowing in 1976, among other sports and events.

Furthermore, not all victorious Eastern Bloc Olympians received negative reactions from Western audiences. At the 1972 Munich Summer Olympics, Soviet gymnast Olga Korbut emerged as the star of the Games. As mentioned above, Olympic women's gymnastics had previously been considered a muscle-inducing, masculine activity. Korbut and her successors helped feminize the sport with their small statures and acrobatic routines.[50] In 1972, Korbut earned three gold medals and one silver. While all of her performances were impressive and dynamic, she gained the most recognition on the uneven bars, where she debuted the "Korbut Flip." This was a difficult routine whereby she did a back flip from the high-bar before re-grasping the lower-bar. Korbut's diminutive-but-powerful physique helped her gain international celebrity.

However, a tragedy that occurred during the Games muted some of the celebrations for her and all Olympians. Members of the terrorist group Black September infiltrated the Olympic Village during the second week of the Olympics. They killed two Israeli athletes onsite and took nine others hostage. After a foiled rescue attempt, the remaining nine Israeli Olympians were killed. Despite the magnitude of the tragedy, the IOC determined that the Games would continue.

Women made strides four years later at the 1976 Montreal Olympics. Romanian gymnast Nadia Comăneci won three gold medals and one silver, including an unprecedented perfect score on the uneven bars. Western audiences adored the "tiny, big-eyed Romanian schoolgirl."[51] Women's basketball, handball, and rowing debuted, creating more medal opportunities claimed by Eastern European competitors. Led by the seven-foot-center Uljana Semjonova, the Soviet Union earned the first gold medal in women's basketball, outscoring opponents by an average of thirty-one points per game. The nation also won the first gold medal in women's handball. Bulgaria, East Germany, the Soviet Union, and Romania claimed fifteen of the eighteen new medals in women's rowing.

Uljana Semjonova being boxed out by Stefania Passaro, 1982.
Wikimedia Commons.

Despite Eastern Bloc sport leaders' best efforts, true equality remained unachieved during the Cold War. Soviet officials attempted to require gender parity through the rulebooks. In 1955, Andrianov proposed changing Rule 29, "Participation of Women," to indicate that the IOC include women in any sport that held a women's world championship. The IOC discussed the proposal in 1958 but delayed a vote until after the 1960 Rome Games. At the 1961 Athens Session, Andrianov again proposed "Women are allowed to compete in all sports recognized by the IOC in which it is provided by the rules of the International Federation concerned." It was defeated, 26-2. He nevertheless continued to fight for women's opportunities at the Olympics and questioned the IOC's commitment to gender equality. At the 1967 Tehran IOC Session, Andrianov unsuccessfully argued that "Declaring the principle of equality for men and women in sport, the IOC, at the same time, restricts women's participation in the Olympic Games."[52] It was not until 1991 that the IOC required all sports applying to join the Olympics have female competitors. The Soviet Union increased opportunities for women, but did not attain parity.

Andrianov also pointed out that stark gender inequalities existed within the IOC governance structure. At the time, women were severely underrepresented at all levels of the Olympic Movement, not just as athletes. The IOC membership and executive board did not have a single female representative. Likewise, one account estimated that women held between zero and one percent of all leadership positions within the international federations and national governing bodies in 1980.[53] One of the few exceptions in female Olympic leadership was French swimmer and Olympic administrator Monique Berlioux. An Olympian who competed in 1948 in the 100m backstroke, she was named the IOC's media chief in 1967 before being appointed the Director of the IOC four years later. The 1971 appointment made her the highest-ranking woman in the Olympic Movement at the time. According to scholar Laura F. Chase, "she was the first women to significantly influence the operations of the IOC."[54] Despite her behind-the-scenes authority, the IOC membership remained an all-male group until 1981.

Conclusion

Cold War tensions reached a crescendo in 1980. The Soviet presence in Afghanistan led the United States to boycott the 1980 Moscow Summer Games. In total, sixty-five countries refused to compete, including the United States' Western allies Canada, Israel, and West Germany. The British Parliament and Prime Minister Margaret Thatcher agreed to boycott the Games; however, the British Olympic Committee defied the government and voted to send athletes. In 1984, the Soviet Union and thirteen other Eastern Bloc countries boycotted the Los Angeles Games in retribution.

Despite the back-to-back boycotts, women in the Cold War Olympics fostered long-lasting changes in women's sport. On the one hand, Eastern European women's athletic supremacy created new opportunities for women in the Olympics. Recognizing the potential for more medals with an expanded female programme, Eastern Bloc leaders successfully lobbied to increase the number of events available to women. Furthermore, the domination of the Eastern Bloc women in the Olympics also encouraged Western officials to elevate women's sport in their home counties. To contend with the Eastern Bloc, Western leaders increased training opportunities and expanded resources for female Olympians.

On the other hand, the gold-medal-performances of the Eastern Bloc women also led to the implementation of restrictive policies. Olympic officials worried that the Eastern European female victors were frauds, which hastened their decision to institute testing protocols. They believed that the athletes were either men posing as women or women using performance-enhancing substances. This led Olympic leaders to introduce compulsory sex control and anti-doping tests at the 1968 Olympics. The significance of women Olympians during the Cold War Olympics can therefore be summed up as generating a tempered acceptance of women's sport, which was undermined by fears about athletes who looked too strong, too powerful, and too muscular.

> ### Discussion Questions
>
> - How did international tensions and geopolitical alliances shape women's sport participation during the Cold War Olympics?
>
> - Should the Eastern Bloc countries, such as the Soviet Union and East Germany, be celebrated for their support of women's sport? Why or why not?
>
> - How did doping concerns and questions about gender merge in the late 1960s? What impact did this have for discussions about femininity and masculinity in sport?
>
> - Can you think of other areas in which women gained increased access during the Cold War era? Did sport create more opportunities for women in the larger society or did social developments increase the involvement of women in sport?

CHAPTER 4

The Limited Liberation of Women in the Olympics by the End of the Century

Women's Olympic Milestones, 1981-2004

1981   Pirjo Häggman of Finland and Flor Isava Fonseca of Venezuela join the International Olympic Committee as its first female members.

274 women (998 men) compete at the Sarajevo Winter Olympics.

Women participate in the 20km cross-country ski race for the first time. Finnish skier Marja-Liisa Hämäläinen finishes first in all three individual cross-country races open to women.

1984

East German speedskater Karin Enke wins two gold medals in the 1,000m and 1,500m. East German women win nine out of the twelve available medals in the sport, which includes four gold, four silver, and one bronze. Soviet speedskater Natalya Glebova wins the other three bronze medals.

Women's Olympic Milestones, 1981-2004, continued...

1984

1,566 women (5,263 men) compete at the Los Angeles Summer Olympics. Women from Antigua and Barbuda, Bhutan, Bolivia, Cayman Islands, the Democratic Republic of the Congo, Egypt, Gabon, the Gambia, Grenada, Honduras, Jordan, Liberia, Mauritius, Papua New Guinea, and Rwanda participate for the first time.

Fourteen Eastern Bloc Countries, including East Germany and the Soviet Union, boycott the Los Angeles Games.

Women compete in several new events: artistic swimming, cycling, rhythmic gymnastics, the marathon, and shooting.

Moroccan hurdler Nawal El Moutawakel is the first woman from an African country to win an Olympic gold medal.

New Zealand archer Neroli Fairhall is the first paraplegic athlete to compete at the Olympics.

US gymnast Mary Lou Retton is the first gymnast from outside Eastern Europe to win the gold medal in the all-around competition. She becomes one of the most famous Olympians in the United States.

1988

301 women (1,122 men) compete at the Calgary Winter Olympics. Alpine skier Claudina Rossel is the first woman from Andorra and Željka Čižmešija is the first woman from Croatia at the Games.

Women's Olympic Milestones, 1981-2004, continued...

Dutch speed skater Yvonne van Gennip wins three gold medals at the Calgary Games.

1988 2,194 women (6,197 men) compete at the Seoul Olympics. Women from Algeria, Aruba, Burkina Faso, Cook Islands, Equatorial Guinea, Guam, Monaco, Myanmar, Nepal, Saint Vincent and the Grenadines, Sri Lanka, Suriname, Tonga, and Vanuatu participate for the first time.

1991 The International Olympic Committee requires all new sports applying for Olympic recognition to include women.

488 women (1,313 men) compete at the Albertville Winter Olympics. Alpine skier Nataša Bokal is the first woman from Slovenia at the Olympics.

Women compete in the biathlon and freestyle skiing for the first time.

1992 2,704 women (6,652 men) compete at the Barcelona Summer Olympics. Women from Bangladesh, Belize, Bosnia Herzegovina, the Central Africa Republic, Chad, Croatia, Guinea, Lesotho, Maldives, Namibia, and Paraguay participate for the first time.

Women compete in judo for the first time.

Women's Olympic Milestones, 1981-2004, continued...

1992

Long-distance runner Derartu Tulu is the first Ethiopian woman to win a gold medal in the 10,000m race.

Thirty-four countries did not include a woman on their Olympic teams.

1994

522 women (1,215 men) compete at the Lillehammer Winter Olympics. Women from Belarus, the Czech Republic, Kazakhstan, Kyrgyzstan, the Republic of Moldova, the Russian Federation, Slovakia, Ukraine, and Uzbekistan participate for the first time.

Uzbekistan freestyle skier Lina Cheryazova wins the gold medal in aerials. She is the country's first medal winner at a Winter Games.

1996

3,523 women (6,797 men) compete at the Atlanta Summer Olympics. Women from American Samoa, Armenia, Azerbaijan, Burundi, Cape Verde, Comoros, Dominica, Eswatini, Georgia, Niger, North Macedonia, Pakistan, Saint Kitts and Nevis, Saint Lucia, São Tomé and Príncipe, Samoa, Serbia and Montenegro, Solomon Islands, Tajikistan, and Turkmenistan participate for the first time.

Women compete in beach volleyball, football (soccer), and softball for the first time. Brazilian athletes Sandra Pires and Jackie Silva win gold in beach volleyball. The US teams win gold medals in football and softball.

Women's Olympic Milestones, 1981-2004, continued...

1996 Long-distance runner Josia Thugwane is the first Black South African woman to win a gold medal in the marathon.

787 women (1,389 men) compete at the Nagano Winter Olympics.

1998 Women compete in curling, ice hockey, and snowboarding for the first time. The Canadian team wins the gold medal in curling, the US team wins the gold medal in ice hockey, and US athlete Kelly Clark wins the women's halfpipe.

4,069 women (6,582 men) compete at the Sydney Summer Olympics. Women from Bahrain, Djibouti, Eritrea, the Federated States of Micronesia, Guinea Bissau, Iraq, Mauritania, Nauru, Palau, Palestine, Somalia, Sudan, Togo, and Yemen participate for the first time.

2000

Women compete in several new events: modern pentathlon, taekwondo, triathlon, trampoline, and weightlifting.

Sprinter Cathy Freeman is the first Indigenous Australian to win a gold medal.

2002 886 women (1,513 men) compete at the Salt Lake City Winter Olympics.

Women's Olympic Milestones, 1981-2004, continued...

2002

Alpine skier Janica Kostelić wins three gold medals and a silver, the first Winter Olympic medals for an athlete from Croatia.

Speedskater Yang Yang wins two gold medals, the first Winter Olympic medals for an athlete from the People's Republic of China.

2004

4,329 women (6,296 men) compete at the Athens Summer Olympics. Women from Afghanistan, Botswana, Kiribati, Kuwait, and Timor Leste participate for the first time.

Women compete in freestyle wrestling for the first time.

German kayaker Birgit Fischer wins a gold and silver medal. She becomes the first person to win two or more medals in five different Games.

Female Olympians had new prospects in the 1980s, 1990s and early 2000s. The women's liberation movement in the 1970s that had helped women gain new financial, legal, and political rights similarly boosted female Olympians' progress. Women's rights leaders pioneered new policies and laws that ushered in an era of expanded participation in physical activity and sport, particularly in Europe and North America. Girls and women took to the courts, fields, and pitches in unprecedented numbers. In 1972, women constituted only 14.8 percent of Olympians at the Summer Games; the number doubled to 28.9 percent at the 1992 Olympics. Women also gained new roles in Olympic leadership. When Pirjo Häggman of Finland and Flor Isava Fonseca of Venezuela joined the International Olympic Committee (IOC) in 1981, they ended an 87-year-long tradition of the IOC as "one of the most exclusive all-male clubs in the world."[1]

However, the progress women achieved in the Olympics by the end of the century was limited and incomplete. Not all women experienced progress at the same rates. Athletes from some countries gained greater access to sport than athletes from other countries. Even on a national level, some competitors reaped the benefits of the women's liberation movement more than others did. In addition, despite gaining new opportunities to display their talents, women were often applauded more for their sex appeal than their athleticism. The sexualization of female athletes undercut their abilities. Finally, the strides women achieved in participation opportunities were not mirrored in leadership positions. Though women broke into the ranks, they remained underrepresented in most decision-making roles. Women in the Olympics at the end of the century can therefore again be summarized as achieving limited progress.

Women's Liberation in Sport

After the Second World War, Western women continued to experience economic, political, and social disenfranchisement. They typically earned less than men, held fewer elected leadership positions, and were discouraged from participating competitively in physical activities. To combat these inequities, women outlined strategies to achieve economic, legal, and social equality. Pioneers demanded an end to employment discrimination, improved control over reproduction, and access to public spaces. Despite fracturing along lines of ability, race, class, and sexuality, the so-called second-wave of the women's liberation movement sparked significant changes in these areas during the late 1960s and early 1970s. Table 4.1 shows milestones achieved in women's sports in the 1970s. By the end of the decade, "a generation of Western women came of age influenced by feminism to expect equal opportunities."[2] Women similarly demanded equal access to sport, including at the Olympics.

Table 4.1 1970s Milestones in Women's Sports

1970	The German Football Association ended its ban on women's football (soccer)
1970	US jockey Diane Crump became the first woman to ride in the Kentucky Derby
1970	Federation of Independent European Female Football organized the "Coppa del Mondo"
1972	Title IX was signed into law in the United States
1973	US tennis player Billie Jean King defeated Bobby Riggs in the "Battle of the Sexes"

1974	Spanish bull fighter Angela Hernandez won a three-year court battle that ended the prohibition against women in the ring, which had been in place since 1908
	Ladies Gaelic Football Association was founded in Ireland
1975	Junko Tabei of Japan became the first woman to reach the summit of Mount Everest
1976	Romanian gymnast Nadia Comăneci earned the first perfect 10 in the Olympics
	Canadian shooter Susan Nattrass became the first woman to compete in Olympic trap shooting
1979	Women overturned a Brazilian law that barred them from participating in baseball, beach soccer, martial arts, rugby, soccer, water polo, and weightlifting
	Norwegian runner Grete Waitz became the first woman to run a marathon in under 2.5 hours

The focus on women's rights encouraged leaders in some countries to outline new policies and laws to increase female participation in sports. For example, connected to the larger women's movement in Canada, the Royal Commission on the Status of Women was created in 1967 to "inquire into and report upon the status of women" in the country. The group identified eight categories of critical issues for women, which ranged from inequalities in the economy to education. Under education, the commission highlighted the underrepresentation of girls in school sport. It therefore recommended in 1970 that provinces and territories review policies "to ensure that school programmes provide girls with equal opportunities with boys to participate in athletic and sports activities."[3] Canadian athletes also started to call for equal opportunities, "pointing to the woefully unequal opportunities they enjoyed in comparison with men."[4] In 1974, Olympians Petra Burka, Abby Hoffman, and Marion Lay organized the National Conference on Women in Sport to help achieve parity. Other advocates formed the Canadian Association for the Advancement of Women (CAAWS) in 1981, a non-governmental agency that sought to ensure gender equality in Canadian sport.[5] Finally, the addition of the Canadian Charter of Rights and Freedoms into the Constitution of Canada in 1982 prohibited discrimination on the basis of sex, which thereby provided girls and women an avenue to address sex discrimination in sport. These factors helped increase the number of women who participated in Canadian sport, including at the Olympic level. For example, only 50 women (158 men) competed for Canada at the 1972 Summer Olympics; by 1992, the number more than doubled to 116 women (179 men).

A similar law in the United States opened the door to girls' and women's participation in sport. Title IX of the 1972 Education Amendments prohibited discrimination on the basis of sex in federally funded educational programs. Supporters of the US law initially saw it as a way to provide women equal access to higher education, reduce sexual harassment in educational settings, and eliminate sex discrimination in schools.[6] However, its most long-lasting consequence was to spark unprecedented growth in the number of girls and women competing in US sport. Title IX required schools to provide women with equitable financial assistance, funding, and participation opportunities on athletic teams. It therefore significantly increased the number of girls and women who played sport. "Growing up in the time of Title IX," US Olympian Jackie Joyner-Kersee reflected in 2012, "I got a front-row seat to so many great moments in women's sports."[7] For example, in 1972, the year Title IX was enacted, approximately 16,000 women participated in university sports; by 2014, the number increased to over 200,000.[8] This helped increase the number of women who represented the United States at the Olympics. At the 1972 Summer Olympics, only 84 of the

400 US Olympians were women. The number increased to 190 (34.9 percent of Team USA) twenty years later. With growing social and legal support, women around the world advanced in the Olympics.

Women's Olympic Strides

Such changes in attitudes, policies, and laws helped women gain Olympic prospects. By the end of the century, women's involvement in the Olympic Movement expanded in three ways. First, the IOC increased the number of competitions available to female Olympians. Women participated in over twenty new sports and disciplines by the end of the century, including in activities previously considered too physically taxing for them, such as judo and the marathon. Second, in line with the expanded Olympic Programme, the number of female Olympians increased. By the beginning of the twenty-first century, women constituted almost 40 percent of athletes during the Summer and Winter Games. Third, women leaders organized and fought for female representation in decision-making positions. They joined boards and committees that were previously composed entirely of men, including the IOC Executive Board and IOC Session.

At almost every Olympic Games during the last quarter of the twenty-first century, the IOC added new sports and/or disciplines for women. Olympic officials and local organizers introduced these new opportunities for several reasons. One, the Soviet pushed for an expanded women's program during the Cold War (discussed in chapter three). Two, US administrator Avery Brundage retired from the IOC presidency in 1972. Throughout his twenty-year-term, he resisted the expansion of the women's Olympic programme. For example, as the IOC Vice President in 1949, Brundage suggested "women's events should be confined to those appropriate for women; swimming, tennis, figure skating, and fencing, but certainly not shot-putting." His views limited the advancement of women's sport during his tenure as IOC president.[9] Three, changes forged by the women's liberation movement sparked an expansion of athletic opportunities. Women competed in a variety of new individual and team sports, shown in Table 4.2. They demonstrated prowess and strength in competitions previously believed to be too grueling for women.

Table 4.2 The Addition of Women's Sports at the Olympics, 1976-2004

Olympics	Sports Added for Women
1976 Montreal Summer Olympics	Basketball Handball Rowing
1980 Moscow Summer Olympics	Field Hockey
1984 Los Angeles Summer Olympics	Artistic Swimming Cycling Shooting
1988 Seoul Summer Olympics	Sailing Table Tennis
1992 Albertville Winter Olympics	Biathlon Freestyle Skiing
1992 Barcelona Summer Olympics	Badminton Judo
1996 Atlanta Olympics	Beach Volleyball Football/Soccer Softball
1998 Nagano Winter Olympics	Curling Ice Hockey Snowboarding

2000 Sydney Summer Olympics	Modern Pentathlon Taekwondo Triathlon Weightlifting
2002 Salt Lake City Winter Olympics	Bobsleigh Skeleton
2004 Athens Summer Olympics	Wrestling

The introduction of the women's marathon at the 1984 Los Angeles Olympics is a helpful example that shows the obstacles Olympians had to overcome to gain inclusion. Unfounded concerns about women's distance running had existed since the beginning, as exemplified in the 800m at the 1928 Olympics (discussed in chapter two). As previously mentioned, the IOC halted women's participation in certain races due to false reports about their supposed inabilities. Olympic officials returned the 800m to the programme in 1960, where it was the longest discipline open to women until 1972, when the IOC introduced the 1,500m. Men had run the marathon since 1896, without ever having to prove their physical aptitude. For decades, Olympic leaders cited disputed medical ideas about the unsuitability of women's bodies as evidence to ban them from competition. "I wouldn't give permission to run a marathon," said US Olympic Coach Dr. Nell Jackson. "I'm very concerned about the effect of these long distances on females."[10] Runners had to combat these prejudices to gain access.

In connection with the larger women's rights movement, women runners advocated and organized. As sport scholar Jaime Schultz notes, they "combined physical activity with political activism to demonstrate that women were capable of far more than the general public imagined."[11] Women marathoners like Monika Boers (Netherlands), Roberta Gibb (United States), Dale Greig

(Scotland), Anni Pede (West Germany), Arlene Pieper (United States), Mildred Sampson (New Zealand), and Kathrine Switzer (United States), among many others, ran marathons, effectively challenging ideas about female frailty. Runners also formed groups, such as the International Runners Committee, to lobby for the expansion of running opportunities. After the IAAF announced that all international marathon events would include a women's race in 1980, the IOC said it needed "more medico-scientific research studies and experiences" before it could include the event at the Olympics.[12] Medical experts quickly reported that ideas about women's inability to run the marathon were rooted in stereotypes, not fact. The IOC eventually approved the marathon in 1981, with US runner Joan Benoit setting a world record at the event's inaugural debut in 1984. It was the fastest women's marathon in history, with nine competitors finishing below the 2:30 mark.

Los Angeles 1984 Olympic Games, Athletics, Marathon Women – Joan Benoit (USA) 1st at the finish. Courtesy of the International Olympic Committee.

These obstacles were not exclusive to the Olympic marathon. Concerns about female Olympians supposed inferior capabilities slowed the addition of women into the Olympics. As scholar Cecile Houry writes, every time women requested inclusion in a sport or event, they "had to prove that they were not only interested but also physically competent."[13] And the more masculine the event, the longer it took the IOC to add women.[14] Women did not participate in the 3,000m steeplechase until 2008, boxing until 2012, ski jumping until 2014, and sprint and slalom canoeing until 2020/2021. As of the 2022 Beijing Winter Olympics, women still do not compete in the 50km race walk, decathlon, Nordic combined, or Greco-Roman wrestling.

Despite this inequality, the number of women participating in the Olympics increased, almost reaching equality by the 2020/2021 Olympics. By the turn of the century, the number of female Olympians reached 38 percent in the Summer Games and 37 percent in the Winter Games. Table 4.3 shows this trend over time.

Table 4.3 Percent of Male and Female Athletes at the Summer Olympics, 1968-2020

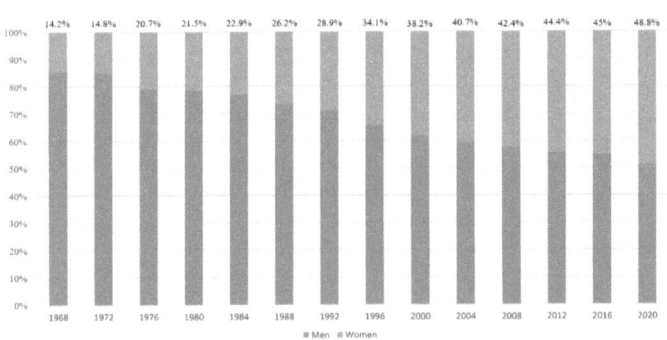

Individual National Olympic Committees (NOCs) also made progress. For example, at the 1968 Mexico City Summer Olympics, five women competed for Nigeria, all in track and field. By 2000, the number of Nigerian female Olympians increased to twenty-two, competing in track and field, judo, swimming, table tennis, and weightlifting. Similar increases occurred around the world. Table 4.4 shows the number of women who competed for the top two medal producing Olympic delegations from each world region in 1968 compared to 2000.[15]

Table 4.4. Women in Top Two Medal Producing Olympic Delegations from Each World Region, 1968 Compared to 2000

Country	1968 Summer Olympics			2000 Summer Olympics		
	No. of Women	% of Women	Total Number of Athletes	No. of Women	% of Women	Total Number of Athletes
Argentina	5	5.6%	89	45	10.9%	413
Australia	24	18.8%	128	276	44.7%	617
Brazil	3	3.9%	76	92	46.5%	198
Canada	28	20.1%	139	144	49%	294
Costa Rica	1	5.6%	18	2	40%	5
Cuba	14	13.9%	101	82	35.8%	229
Great Britain	50	28.6%	175	129	41.6%	310
Jamaica	5	20%	25	26	54.2%	48
Japan	25	14.6%	171	110	41.4%	266
Kenya	3	7.7%	39	23	41.1%	56
New Zealand	5	9.6%	52	70	47.6%	147
Panama	0	0%	16	2	33.3%	6
Republic of China	Did not compete			180	66.4%	271
South Africa	Did not compete			38	29.9%	127
Soviet Union/Russia	66	21.2%	312	194	44.6%	435
United States	83	23.3%	357	253	43.2%	586

Although many Olympic delegations achieved near parity by the end of the century, some continued to include only male Olympians.

Finally, women also worked for increased representation in Olympic leadership positions. For over eighty years, the IOC membership was exclusively male. It was not until 1981 that Flor Isava Fonseca and Pirjo Häggman joined the IOC as members, with Isava Fonseca later serving on the IOC Executive Board as the first woman in 1990. Concerned about the continued underrepresentation of women in Olympic governance, female leaders from around the world organized to address the issue.[16]

91th IOC Session in Lausanne, 1986 – Flor Isava Fonseca, IOC member (VEN). Courtesy of the International Olympic Committee.

In 1994, the Great Britain Sports Council hosted the "Women, Sport, and the Challenge of Change" conference in Brighton, United Kingdom. During the conference, 280 attendees from 82 countries discussed issues women faced in sports. Importantly, the conference established the Brighton Declaration, an international treaty that sought to achieve gender parity in all aspects of sport. One of the ten principles specifically called on signees to "increase the number of women coaches, advisers, decision makers, officials, administrators and sports personnel at all levels."[17] The IOC signed the Brighton Declaration and started its efforts to achieve equality in the Olympic Movement. It hosted the first IOC World Conference on Women and Sport in 1996, during which Olympic leaders recommended international federations and National Olympic Committees (NOCs) "take into consideration" gender equality in leadership roles. IOC President Juan Antonio Samaranch proposed the following year that women be afforded at least ten percent representation in IOC decision-making positions by 2000. The efforts helped women gain new positions as Olympic leaders.

91st IOC Session in Lausanne, 1986 – Pirjo Wilmi Häggman, IOC member (FIN). Courtesy of the International Olympic Committee.

Women's Olympic Hurdles

Despite these achievements, progress was limited in several ways. First, the advancements made in Olympic participation was uneven. Women from some countries gained greater Olympic opportunities than women from other countries did. Disparities also existed within individual countries. Second, for the athletes who did reach the Olympic stage, audiences frequently fixated on their appearances. The sexualization of female Olympians undercut their athleticism. Finally, women made minimal improvement in gaining decision-making positions. At the end of the century, men still dominated the ranks of Olympic organizations.

Uneven Olympic Participation

Female Olympians gained access to the Games in varying degrees. As shown above in Table 4.3, the total number of female Olympians more than doubled by the end of the century. Despite the progress, some Olympic delegations continued to be composed entirely of men. In the 1988 Seoul Olympics, 26.3 percent of Olympic teams did not include a female athlete. Table 4.5 shows the number of Olympic delegations that participated from 1988 to 2000 without women.

Table 4.5 Number of Countries that Did Not Include Female Athletes at the Summer Olympics, 1988-2000[18]

	Countries without a Female Athlete	
	Number	Percent
1988 Seoul	42	26.3%
1992 Barcelona	34	20.1%
1996 Atlanta	28	14.2%
2000 Sydney	9	4.5%

As mentioned above, the number of women who competed for European, Oceania, North American, and South American countries increased significantly by the 2000 Sydney Olympics. For example, from 1972 to 1992, the number of women who represented France at the Olympics grew from thirty to ninety-eight. Over the same period, the representation of women on the Brazilian Olympic team increased from 3.7 percent to 27.5 percent. Some nations, such as Australia and the Soviet Union, neared gender parity by the end of the century. In contrast, women from some Asian, African, and Caribbean Olympic teams remained underrepresented as Olympians. Table 4.6 lists the thirty-four countries that did not include a female athlete at the 1992 Barcelona Games, arranged by Olympic geographic region. The nine countries in bold text did not include women in 1992, 1996, and 2000. Botswana, Kuwait, and Libyan Arab Jamahiriya added women in 2004; the British Virgin Islands, Oman, United Arab Emirates, and Yemen added women in 2008; and Qatar and Saudi Arabia added women in 2012.

Table 4.6 Countries that Did Not Include Female Athletes at the 1992 Summer Olympics.[19]

Geographical Region	#	Countries
Africa	11	**Botswana**, Burkina Faso, Djibouti, Gambia, **Libyan Arab Jamahiriya**, Mauritania, Niger, Sudan, Swaziland, Tanzania, and Togo
Asia	13	Bahrain, Iraq, Islamic Republic of Iran, **Kuwait**, Lao People's Democratic Republic, Lebanon, Malaysia, **Oman**, Pakistan, **Qatar**, **Saudi Arabia**, **United Arab Emirates**, and **Yemen**
Europe	0	--
Oceania	4	American Samoa, Cook Islands, Solomon Islands, and Western Samoa
Pan-America	6	**British Virgin Islands**, Cayman Islands, Haiti, Panama, Trinidad and Tobago, and Uruguay

Western audiences criticized the absence of women at the Olympics. For example, Atlanta Plus, a European-based feminist group with representatives from Belgium, France, Germany, and Sweden, wrote a letter to the IOC after the 1992 Summer Olympics. It expressed concern that over thirty countries had not included women at the Barcelona Games. The group requested the IOC ban any nation that did not include female Olympians from the 1996 Atlanta Games. "Discrimination of any kind is contrary to the spirit of the Olympics," argued French attorney Linda Weil-Cureil. "It is contrary to the Olympic Charter." Atlanta Plus likened the exclusion of women to the exclusion of Black athletes from South African teams, which led the IOC to bar the country from the Games for almost thirty years. The IOC disagreed. "For us it's not an issue," said IOC general director Francois Carrard. "It is an attack against religion for political purposes."[20] At the 1996 Atlanta Olympics, twenty-eight delegations did not include women.

NOCs did not include women on their delegations for several reasons. It is true that in some of the countries, Islamic leaders interpreted women's sport as incompatible with religious values. For example, after the Iranian Revolution in 1979, the newly established Islamic Republic of Iran briefly discontinued women's competitions. Because the government required gender segregation in public spaces, religious leaders saw the presence of male coaches, officials, and spectators in women's sport as a problem.[21] Women had competed for Iran at the 1964 and 1976 Summer Olympics. After the revolution, the Islamic Republic of Iran NOC did not send a delegation again until 1988 and Iranian women did not compete until 1996. Female athletes in Qatar faced several similar barriers to their participation in sport, including cultural norms regarding gender segregation, lack of acceptance from family members, and prohibitions about attire.[22] Qatari male Olympians first competed in 1984; Qatari female Olympians first competed in 2012.

Nawal El Moutawakel after winning the women's 400m hurdles at the 1984 Summer Olympics. Wikimedia Commons.

However, this Western interpretation presented a generalized view of Islam and ignored the successes of Muslim women at the Olympics. Islamic feminists argued that some religious leaders misused Islamic teachings to subjugate women, including in sport. They pointed out that Islam promotes health and encourages men and women to engage in physical activity.[23] This viewpoint helped women from Muslim-majority countries reach the Olympic stage. In 1984, Moroccan hurdler Nawal El Moutawakel became the first woman from a Muslim-majority country—and first woman from an African country—to win an Olympic gold medal. She later became a member of the IOC and in 2008 became the first woman from a Muslim-majority country to join the IOC Executive Board. At the 1992 Barcelona Olympics, Indonesian Olympian Susi Susanti became the first woman to win a gold medal from the world's most populous Muslim country.[24]

This view of Islam also ignored the obstacles the Olympic structure created for Muslim women. Certain Olympic requirements about apparel, facilities, and timing were incompatible with Islamic beliefs. Uniform regulations prevented some Muslim women's participation due to religious beliefs in body modesty. For example, when beach volleyball debuted at the Olympics in 1996, the rules required female Olympians to wear bathing suits or bikinis. As scholars Tansin Benn and Symeon Dagkas explain, such clothing requirements were "tantamount to excluding Muslim athletes and exacerbating the wider prejudice and discrimination Muslim sports women can face"[25] The public nature of the Olympics also presented potential obstacles for some Muslim women who required sex-segregated spaces. Furthermore, the Olympics occasionally occurred during Ramadan, a religious observance that requires a month of fasting, which posed unique challenges for Muslim athletes. Iranian women's right activist Faezeh Hashemi highlighted these issues at the IOC World Conference on Women and Sport in 1996. "Muslim women are ignored because of their moralities as stated in their religion," she argued. "There are 500 million Muslim women in the world, one-fourth of the world's female population, who cannot do sport in the existing conditions. What is the problem with having competitions in accordance with our conditions? . . . The IOC belongs to all the people of the world, not to specific groups in the world or groups as a majority."[26]

The focus on the non-participation of women from certain countries also overshadowed issues of representation at the national level. Female Olympians of different ethnic, racial, and class backgrounds experienced different levels of access, opportunities, and resources in sport. For example, Title IX in the United States overwhelmingly benefited white, middle-class girls and women.[27] This led to an overrepresentation of white women on Team USA. Similar patterns existed in other Western countries. For example, an Indigenous woman did not make the Australian

Olympic team until 1992, when Samantha Riley won bronze in the 100m breaststroke and Cathy Freeman competed in track. Freeman became the first Indigenous Australian to win a gold medal at the 2000 Sydney Olympics. A 2017 report on Australian, Canadian, British, and US Olympians found that 81.7 percent of Summer athletes, and 94.9 percent of Winter athletes, at the 2014 and 2016 Olympics, respectively, were white.[28] The benefits achieved by the women's liberation movement were thus uneven at best.

Sexualization of Olympians

In addition to securing uneven gains in athletic opportunities, women were also sexualized. Audiences, commentators, and sponsors celebrated their looks more than their athleticism. Although the sexualization of female Olympians started decades earlier, it heightened in the 1980s and 1990s as the Olympics became increasingly commercialized. This sexualization undercut female Olympians' athleticism.

The Olympics became increasingly commercialized in the 1980s, with the 1984 Olympics serving as an important milestone. For the first time in the modern era, the Los Angeles Olympics earned a financial surplus. The IOC accrued significant income from exclusive television deals and LA Olympic Committee Chair Peter Ueberroth introduced corporate sponsorships into the Games. The result was a $215 million dollar profit. As the Olympics became increasingly entwined with corporate interests, the IOC loosened its amateur regulations. Olympic leaders had prohibited Olympians from accepting endorsements or playing professionally throughout most of its history. In 1971, the IOC permitted sponsorships for the first time, allowing athletes to sign deals with sport organizations and private businesses. In 1986, it allowed international federations to determine eligibility standards, opening the door for professionals. For example, after the International Basketball Federation (FIBA) voted to permit professionals in 1989, the US "Dream Team," composed primarily of National Basketball Association players, defeated opponents by an average of forty-four points in route to the 1992 gold medal. Although female Olympians did not sign as lucrative of deals as male Olympians, they did appear in commercials, on merchandise, and as spokespersons. For example, after becoming the first US gymnast to win the all-around in 1984, Mary Lou Retton signed numerous endorsement agreements, including with McDonald's, Vidal Sassoon, and Wheaties.

Yet, Olympians who fit normative expectations of femininity earned more than those who did not. In other words, the tall, slender, conventionally attractive (and oftentimes white and Western) female Olympians received media coverage and signed deals. For instance, in explaining why Vidal Sassoon, a hair product company, wanted Retton to endorse its products, spokesperson Jacqueline Applebaum noted that Retton was "very clean, very wholesome and very all-American." Columnist Eric Schmitt added that her "appeal apparently stems as much from her dazzling smile as from her athletic prowess."[29] The undermining of athletic ability was found across media outlets and sponsorship deals. One study examined images from the 1984 and 1988 Olympics in Major North American magazines and found notable contrasts between the photographs of male and female Olympians. The women were photographed in ways that bore a "striking resemblance to those of women in soft-core pornography." Images showed them with "pinup" facial expressions; situated in sexualized positions; or zoomed in on their pelvic areas or buttocks.[30] Such coverage afforded the women celebrity status, but in a way that downgraded their athleticism.

Limitations in Leadership

The addition of Häggman and Isava Fonseca to the IOC in 1981 was an important moment. Their presence ended the tradition of only men serving on the IOC, started by Coubertin in 1894. Speaking before the 84th IOC Session that year, IOC President Juan Antonio Samaranch described the election as a "revolution," which he hoped would "incite all other members of the Olympic family to consider the question of women's participation and . . . . form a powerful invitation to those International Federations which have not yet given a place to female administrators."[31]

However, the "revolution" fell short as progress in securing leadership positions for other women in the Olympic Movement remained slow. From 1987 to 1995, the IOC added fifty-four representatives, only three of whom were women: Mary Alison Glen-Haig of Great Britain, Princess Nora of Liechtenstein, and Anita DeFrantz of the United States. Female representation in the IOC membership hovered around 7 percent in the 1990s.[32] Women also continued to be underrepresented on the IOC Executive Board, the smaller, more powerful group within the Olympic governance structure. Isava Fonseca was elected the first woman to the IOC Executive Board in 1990; DeFrantz was elected the first female IOC Vice-President in 1997.[33] Gaps were even more pronounced within international federations, NOCs, and as coaches.

Conclusion

US Olympians and sister-in-laws Jackie Joyner-Kersee and Florence Griffith Joyner, "Flo-Jo," excelled in track and field at the end of the twentieth century, winning eleven Olympic medals between them. Joyner-Kersee finished second in the heptathlon's 1984 debut, then claimed gold in 1988 and 1992. An additional gold and two bronzes in the long jump rounded out her medal haul. Flo-Jo also won a silver medal in 1984, then earned three gold and an additional silver in 1988 sprint and relay events. The Olympians earned their accolades during a time when women experienced new sporting opportunities, bolstered by the women's liberation movement. This included an expansion of the Olympic programme. For the 1984 Los Angeles Olympics, the IOC introduced artistic swimming, cycling, and rhythmic gymnastics. It also replaced the pentathlon with the heptathlon, and added the 3,000m, 400m hurdles, and marathon races for women. Seven years later, Olympic leaders announced that every new sport introduced into the Olympic Games must include a women's event, further increasing the number of women allowed to compete.

Against this backdrop, Joyner-Kersee and Griffith Joyner shined. However, their appearances received almost as much attention as their accomplishments. Columnists fixated on their looks, especially Flo-Jo's. Florence Griffith had long, colorful fingernails and competed in bright, self-designed, one-legged uniforms. Though she won Olympic medals and set world records, her adornments oftentimes generated more coverage than her athleticism. Reporters repeatedly described her "flamboyant fingernails" and "one-leggers." Furthermore, in comparing Joyner-Kersee and Flo-Jo, US columnist Jay Weiner concluded, "Joyner-Kersee equals athlete. Griffith Joyner equals flash." His comment spoke to the status of female Olympians at the end of the century. They made strides in sport, but audiences continued to praise their "flash" over their athleticism. The significance of women in the Olympics in the later part of the twentieth century is therefore best surmised as expanded athletic and financial opportunities (for some), undermined by sex appeal and continued limitations in leadership.

Discussion Questions

- How did the women's liberation movement affect women's involvement in sport? How did women's involvement in sport affect the women's liberation movement?

- Why are Western gender norms dominant in the Olympic Movement? How can individuals and organizations from other regions challenge such viewpoints?

- What impact did the commercialization of the Olympic Movement have on the presentation of the female body in sport and at the Olympic Games?

- Will the inclusion of women on the decision-making level impact women's participation and representation in the Olympic Movement?

CONCLUSION

Olympic Strides and Hurdles

Women's Olympic Milestones, 2006-2022

2006	960 women (1,548 men) compete at the Turin Winter Olympics.
2008	4,637 women (6,305 men) compete at the Beijing Summer Olympics. Women from the British Virgin Islands, Marshall Islands, Montenegro, Oman, Serbia, Tuvalu, and the United Arab Emirates participate for the first time. Baseball and boxing are the only sports not open to women.
2010	1,043 women (1,536 men) compete at the Vancouver Winter Olympics.
2012	4,774 women (5,992 men) compete at the London Summer Olympics. Women from Brunei Darussalam, the Kingdom of Saudi Arabia, and Qatar participate for the first time.

Women's Olympic Milestones, 2006-2022, continued...

2012	Women compete in boxing for the first time. With baseball dropped from the Olympic program, this is the first Olympics at which women compete in all the events.
2014	1,158 women (1,708 men) compete at the Sochi Winter Olympics.
	Women compete in ski jumping for the first time. German Olympian Carina Vogt wins the first gold medal in the event.
2016	5,059 women (6,000 men) compete at the Rio Olympics. Men and women from Kosovo and South Sudan participate for the first time.
	Women compete in rugby sevens for the first time. The Australian team wins the gold medal.
2018	1,204 women (1,704 men) compete at the PyeongChang Winter Olympics.
2020/ 2021	The Covid-19 pandemic forces the International Olympic Committee to postpone the Summer Olympics until 2021.
	5,486 women (5,988 men) compete at the Tokyo Summer Olympics. Women compete in 3x3 basketball, karate, sport climbing, surfing, and water polo for the first time.

Women's Olympic Milestones, 2006-2022, continued...	
2020/ 2021	Out transgender Olympians compete for the first time.
2022	1,276 women (1,581 men) compete at the Beijing Winter Olympics.

Over one hundred years ago, Pierre de Coubertin and his fellow International Olympic Committee (IOC) members barred women from competing at the 1896 Athens Olympics. They ultimately failed to keep women sidelined entirely as local organizing committees permitted their entrance from the 1900 Paris Games onward. Nevertheless, in establishing the Games as the echelon of male excellence, Coubertin and the mostly male members of the IOC successfully ensured women would continuously have to fight for inclusion in the Olympic Movement. During the early decades of the twenty-first century, the trend continued. The road toward gender equality was one constantly beset by roadblocks.

Female Olympians gained new sporting opportunities in the 2000s. For the first time, women competed in the bobsleigh (2002); freestyle wrestling (2004); BMX cycling, 3000m steeplechase, and 10km swim (2008); ski cross (2010); boxing (2012); ski jumping (2014); rugby sevens (2016); and karate, skateboarding, and surfing (2020). The number of female Olympians also neared parity with male Olympians. Women accounted for 49 percent of athletes at the 2020/2021 Tokyo Summer Olympics and 45 percent of athletes at the 2022 Beijing Winter Olympics.[1] IOC pressure also forced the four remaining National Olympic

Committees that had yet to include women to bring at least one to the 2016 Rio Olympics.

Female leaders also gained new opportunities during the early decades of the century. The IOC's strategic plan, *Olympic Agenda 2020*, included aims for more equitable representation. To reach this goal, in 2018 the IOC approved the *IOC Gender Equality Review Project*. The document outlined ways to improve gender equity in participation, media portrayal, governance structure, and funding.[2] One of the recommendations called on the IOC to achieve "equal representation of women and men" in executive leadership positions by 2024. Due to such efforts, during the 2020/2021 Olympics, women comprised 36.3 percent of the IOC membership and 26.7 percent of the IOC Executive Board.[3]

Yet, as shown throughout this pocketbook, advancements occurred inconsistently. Women in parts of the world gained increased access while others did not. For example, facing pressure from the IOC, the eighteen-person Saudi Arabian delegation included two female athletes in 2012, for the first time in Olympic history. Brunei and Qatar also permitted female Olympians for the first time that year. Yet, the women were significantly outnumbered. For example, at the 2020/2021 Tokyo Summer Olympics, twenty-nine men and two women participated for Saudi Arabia.

Furthermore, expanded opportunities sparked questions about eligibility. Concerns about female Olympians in the new millennium have primarily focused on intersex and transgender (trans) athletes. Intersex is a general term used to describe people born with characteristics—such as anatomy, chromosomal patterns, or genetics—that do not fit neatly into typical notions of male or female bodies. Transgender is an umbrella term that refers to people whose gender identity does not match their sex assigned at birth. Although intersex athletes and trans athletes are different populations with different experiences, sport officials have conflated the two groups and created obstacles to their participation in sport.

The IOC outlined various policies for intersex and trans athletes during the first two decades of the century. It introduced a transgender athlete policy in 2003, the Stockholm Consensus. Trans athletes who wanted to compete in the Olympics had to follow three guidelines: undergo gender affirmation surgery with changes to external genitalia; receive legal recognition of sex; and administer hormone therapy to "minimise gender-related advantages in competitive sport competitions."[4] Critics questioned the relevance of requiring anatomical surgery for sport participation and noted that expenses involved to do so. They also pointed out that legal recognition remained difficult for many trans people to attain in certain parts of the world.[5] Although the IOC claimed it sought to be inclusive, the Stockholm Consensus essentially barred trans athletes. No out trans person competed at the Olympic under the guidelines.

Olympic officials similarly sought to limit the inclusion of intersex athletes. After South African runner Caster Semenya drew international attention at the 2009 World Track and Field Championships, the International Association of Athletics Federations (IAAF), now World Athletics, required she undergo a sex test. The international federation and IOC later introduced new policies focused on women with hyperandrogenism. Hyperandrogenism is a medical condition characterized by higher-than-average, naturally-produced levels of testosterone. In 2011, the IOC introduced its "Regulations on Female Hyperandrogenism" and the IAAF announced parallel "Regulations Governing Eligibility of Females with Hyperandrogenism to Compete in Women's Competition." Those diagnosed needed to undergo various interventions to reduce their testosterone levels as a requirement to compete in the Olympics.

Rio 2016 Olympic Games, Athletics, 800m Women - Semifinal, Caster Semenya (RSA) 1st, Noelie Yarigo (BEN), Kate Grace (USA), Lynsey Sharp (GBR) and Marina Arzamasova (BLR). Courtesy of the International Olympic Committee.

During the 2012 London Games, officials sent four women to France for such treatment.[6] The doctors recommended the Olympians undergo a medical procedure to be able to compete in sport. Opting out of the surgery carried no health risk to the athlete. However, in order to compete, they had to consent. With no other options, the Olympians agreed.

Two years later, Indian runner Dutee Chand faced a similar choice: undergo an unnecessary medical intervention or retire from sport. She instead went public with her situation and challenged the hyperandrogenism policies in the Court of Arbitration for Sport (CAS), an international body responsible for adjudicating issues in sport. CAS found that the IAAF had provided insufficient evidence about the degree of advantage women with high levels of testosterone have over others. The CAS panel suspended the policy for two years.

With the testosterone policy suspended, Semenya and other athletes suspected of having hyperandrogenism were allowed to compete. As noted above, Semenya won gold at the 2016 Rio Olympics. She then claimed a gold and bronze at the 2017 World Championships, and two golds at the 2018 Commonwealth Games.

Also in the interim, the IOC introduced a new policy for trans athletes, the 2015 IOC Consensus Meeting on Sex Reassignment and Hyperandrogenism. The new regulations moved away from surgical interventions and focused on testosterone levels. It allowed trans women to compete so long as they lowered their testosterone levels to 10 nmol/L for at least twelve months prior to competition. As a result, out trans Olympians competed for the first time in Tokyo. Quinn helped Canada win the gold medal in football (soccer); New Zealand's Laurel Hubbard participated in weightlifting; and US BMX Freestyle cyclist Chelsea Wolfe served as a reserve.

Intersex athletes also faced new restrictions in track and field. The IAAF introduced Eligibility Regulations for Female Classification (Athletes with Differences of Sex Development) in April 2018. The new regulations applied only to women who competed on the track in distances from 400m to the mile, including hurdles and combined events over those distances. Competitors in these events were required to keep their hormone level below 5 nmol/L. Members of the medical community advised doctors against following the new protocol, saying it breached medical ethics. World-renowned runners detailed the harms caused by the testosterone thresholds. They reported being subjected to invasive examinations and coerced into medically unnecessary procedures that left them physically unwell. They also described experiencing social stigmatization and negative psychological repercussions, which at times included suicidal thoughts.[7]

After implementing controversial restrictions for both groups centered on hormone levels, the IOC introduced a new policy in 2021. The IOC backtracked from its previous testosterone-based regulations. Olympic leaders released the "IOC Framework on Fairness, Inclusion and Non-Discrimination on the Basis of Gender Identity and Sex Variations." The document provides guidance to sport organizations on how to develop participation standards. It includes ten guiding principles: inclusion, prevention of harm, non-discrimination, fairness, no presumption of advantage, evidenced-based approach, primacy of health and bodily autonomy, stakeholder-centered approach, right to privacy and periodic reviews. It suggests sport organizations should neither use "invasive physical examinations" nor require athletes to "undergo medically unnecessary procedures of treatment" for eligibility purposes. The IOC Framework is merely a suggestion, not a requirement. International Federations are allowed to write their own rules about intersex and transgender athletes. Many federations have therefore introduced different practices for, or outright bans on, intersex and trans athletes.

***

During the 2016 Rio Olympics, Semenya earned gold, Burundi's Francine Niyonsaba earned silver, and Kenya's Margaret Wambui earned bronze in the 800m final. In doing so, Semenya added a second gold medal to her haul[8] and Niyonsaba's silver medal was the second earned by a Burundi competitor at the Olympics. "The field was really good," said Semenya after the race. "It was fantastic to race with such great athletes." For Niyonsaba, she explained, "It is a honour for me and my country to make history. I'm an Olympic medallist, the first one for my country since 1996."[9] Yet, not everyone shared their sentiments.

After crossing the finish line in sixth place, British runner Lynsey

Sharp told the BBC that "everyone can see it's two separate races so there's nothing I can do." Polish fifth-place-finisher Joanna Jozwik was less abstract in her comments. She told *Eurosport* that she was "glad that I'm the first European, and the second White" to finish the race.[10] Sharp's and Jozwik's comments underscore the treatment women experience in the Olympics when they upset gendered and racialized norms. As has been apparent throughout this book, women who challenged prevailing ideas about their place in sport face criticism, resentment, and exclusion.

In other words, women's place in the Olympics has been tenuous from the beginning. When Pierre de Coubertin founded the modern Olympic Movement, he did not include women in his vision. He viewed the Olympics as a way for boys to cultivate manliness and men to demonstrate masculinity. Women as Olympians challenged his plans.

The Olympics therefore remain a preserve of men. Women have yet to reach parity as either athletes or leaders. This is notable in certain areas around the world where social norms conflict with the structure of the Games. Moreover, women who breach gender norms by being too muscular or too successful face suspicion and derision. This extends into the leadership realm where women remain severely underrepresented as decision makers and coaches at all levels.

Throughout the history of the Olympics women have worked for increased opportunities as athletes, equal access to elite sports, and a place in the governance structure. They have made strides, but hurdles remain.

Discussion Questions

- Why do intersex and transgender Olympians face obstacles to their Olympic participation? How is this similar to, and different from, the obstacles cisgender women Olympians faced throughout the history of the Olympics?

- Are mixed-gender competitions beneficial for the development of women's sport or simply a tool to increase the number of women's participants? Do you think some sports will always be gender specific? Why or why not?

- What do you consider to be the main questions and issues concerning gender in sport in the future?

NOTES

Introduction

1. Quoted in: Mark Dyreson, *Making the American Team: Sport, Culture, and the Olympic Experience* (Champaign: University of Illinois Press, 1998), 34.
2. Pierre de Coubertin, "The Women at the Olympic Games," in *Olympism. Selected Writings*, ed. Norbert Müller (Lausanne: International Olympic Committee, 2000), 542-546.
3. John W. Loy, Fiona McLachlan, and Douglas Booth, "Connotations of Female Movement and Meaning," *Olympika: The International Journal of Sports Studies* XVIII (2009): 1-24.
4. Kay Schiller and Christopher Young, *The 1972 Munich Olympics and the Making of Modern Germany* (Berkeley: University of California Press, 2010), 14.
5. Callie B. Maddox, "Under One Banner": The World Baseball Softball Confederation and the Gendered Politics of Olympic Participation," *Sport History Review* 51, no. 1 (2020): 125-144.
6. Maureen M. Smith and Alison Wrynn, *Women in the 2000, 2004, and 2008 Olympic and Paralympic Games: An Analysis of Participation, Leadership and Media Opportunities* (East Meadow: Women's Sport Foundation, 2009).
7. Emily Houghton, Maureen M. Smith, and Lindsay Parks Pieper, *Women in the 2020 Olympic and Paralympic Games: An Analysis of Participation, Leadership, and Media Coverage* (East Meadow: Women's Sport Foundation, 2022).
8. Loy, McLachlan, and Booth, "Connotations of Female Movement and Meaning," 12.

Obstacles to Women's Participation in Sport

1. Information about the first appearances of women came from Olympedia, http://www.olympedia.org/. Contemporary names are used whenever applicable.
2. Maria Isabel Ramos, "Women Playing a Man's Game: Reconstructing Ceremonial and Ritual History of the Mesoamerican Ballgame," (PhD diss., University of California San Diego, 2012), 26.
3. Mike Speak, "Recreation and Sport in Ancient China: Primitive Society to AD 960," in *Sport and Physical Education in China*, eds. James Riordan and Robin Jones (New York: Routledge, 1999), 26.
4. Lara O'Sullivan, "Playing ball in Greek Antiquity," *Greece & Rome* 59, no. 1 (2012): 17-33.
5. Bruce Kidd, "Sports and Masculinity," *Sport in Society* 16, no. 4 (2013): 553-564.
6. Wolfgang Decker, *Sport in der Griechischen Antike* (Hildesheim: arete Verlag, 2012), 106
7. Ibid.
8. Matthew Dillon, *Girls and Women in Classical Greek Religion* (London: Routledge, 2002).
9. Allen Guttmann, "Sports Spectators from Antiquity to the Renaissance," *Journal of Sport History* 8, no. 2 (1981): 5-27.

10. Reet Howell and Maxwell L. Howell, "Women in the Medieval and Renaissance Period: Spectators Only," *Sport History Review* 17, no. 1 (1986), 11-37.
11. Jörg Krieger, "Cotswold, Much Wenlock, Morpeth – 'Olympic Games' before Pierre de Coubertin," in *Olympia. Deutschland – Großbritannien* (Cologne: Carl und Liselott Diem-Archive, 2012), 23-37.
12. Allen Guttmann, *Sports: The First Five Millennia* (Amherst: University of Massachusetts Press, 2007), 68ff.
13. Thomas Hughes, *Tom Brown's School Days* (Chicago and New York: Belford, Clarke & Co, 1886). See also: Richard Holt, *Sport and the British. A Modern History* (Oxford: Clarendon Press, 1989).
14. Kidd, "Sports and Masculinity."
15. Boria Majumdar, "South Asian Sport," in *The Oxford Handbook of Sports History*, eds. Robert Edelman and Wayne Wilson (New York: University of Oxford Press, 2017), 257-272.
16. Susan Cahn, *Coming on Strong: Gender and Sexuality in Twentieth-Century Women's Sport* (Champaign: University of Illinois Press, 1994), 11.
17. Jaime Schultz, *Women's Sports. What Everyone Needs to Know* (New York: Oxford University Press, 2018), 14.
18. Ibid., 15.
19. Jean Williams and Rob Hess, "Women, Football and History: International Perspectives," *The International Journal of the History of Sport* 32, no. 18 (2015), 2116.
20. André Odendaal, "'Neither Cricketers nor Ladies': Towards a History of Women and Cricket in South Africa, 1860s–2000s', *The International Journal of the History of Sport* 28, no. 1 (2011), 116.
21. Allen Gutmann, *Women's Sports: A History* (New York: Columbia University Press, 1991), 101.
22. Cahn, *Coming on Strong*.
23. Jean Williams, "The Fastest Growing Sport? Women's Football in England," *Soccer & Society* 4, no. 2-3 (2003): 112-127.
24. Holt, *Sport and the British*.
25. John Hargreaves, "Sport, Culture and Ideology," in *Sport, Culture and Ideology*, ed. Jennifer Hargreaves (London: Routledge and Kegan Paul, 1982), 38.
26. Holt, *Sport and the British*, 118.
27. Dikaia Chatziefstathiou and Ian Henry, "Hellenism and Olympism: Pierre de Coubertin and the Greek Challenge to the Early Olympic Movement," *Sport in History* 27, no. 1 (2007): 24-43.
28. Quoted in Ana Maria Miragaya, "The Process of Inclusion of Women in the Olympic Games," (PhD diss., Universidade Gama Filho, 2006).
29. Pierre de Coubertin, "The Paris Congress and the Revival of the Olympic Games," in *Olympism. Selected Writings*, ed. Norbert Müller (Lausanne: International Olympic Committee, 2001), 317.
30. Ibid.
31. Thierry Terret, "Pierre de Coubertin (1863-1937): A Proponent of Sporting Masculinity," *Journal of Olympic History*, no. 1 (2013): 4-7.
32. Miragaya, "The Process of Inclusion."
33. Pierre de Coubertin, "The Philosophic Foundation of Modern Olympism," in *Olympism. Selected Writings*, ed. Norbert Müller (Lausanne: International Olympic Committee, 2000), 580-584
34. Coubertin, "The Women at the Olympic Games."
35. Ibid.
36. Thierry Terret, "Pierre de Coubertin (1863-1937)."
37. Ibid.

38. Bill Maloon, *The 1904 Olympic Games. Results for All Competitors in All Events, with Commentary* (Jefferson: McFarland, 1999).
39. Else Trangbæk, "Gender in Modern Society: Femininity, Gymnastics and Sport," *The International Journal of the History of Sport* 14, no. 3 (1997): 136-156.
40. Quoted in: Trangbæk, "Gender in Modern Society," 147.
41. In Sheila Mitchell, "Women's Participation in the Olympic Games 1900-1926," *Journal of Sport History* 4, no. 2 (1977): 212.
42. Maylon Hanold, *Women in Sports. A Reference Handbook* (Santa Barbara: ABC-CLIO, 2018).
43. Helen Lenskyj, "Physical Activity for Canadian Women, 1890-1930: Media Views," in *From "Fair Sex" to Feminism. Sport and the Socialization of Women in the Industrial and Post-industrial Eras*, eds. Joe Mangan and Roberta Park (London: Frank Cass, 1987), 208-231.
44. Dikaia Chatziefstathiou, "Reading Baron Pierre de Coubertin: Issues of Gender and Race," *Aethlon* XXV (2008): 2.
45. Mitchell, "Women's Participation."

Fights for Inclusion

1. Jörg Krieger, Michele Krech, and Lindsay Parks Pieper, "'Our Sport': The Fight for Control of Women's International Athletics," *The International Journal of the History of Sport* 37, no. 5-6 (2020): 451-472.
2. Norbert Müller, *One Hundred Years of Olympic Congresses 1894-1994* (Lausanne: International Olympic Committee, 1994).
3. Jennifer Hargreaves, *Sporting Females: Critical Issues in the History and Sociology of Women's Sports* (London: Routledge, 1994), 131-133.
4. Jean Williams, *The History of Women's Football* (Barnsley: Pen and Sword, 2022).
5. Hajo Bernett, *Leichtathletik im geschichtlichen Wandel* (Schorndof: Hofmann, 1987).
6. Fiona Skillen, *Women, Sport and Modernity in Interwar Britain* (Oxford: Peter Lang, 2013), 1. Also see: Hargreaves, *Sporting Females*, 125.
7. Louise Mead Tricard, *American Women's Track and Field: A History, 1895 through 1980* (Jefferson, North Carolina: McFarland, 1996).
8. Mary H. Leigh and Thérèse M. Bonin, "The Pioneering Role of Madame Alice Milliat and the FSFI in Establishing International Trade and Field Competition for Women," *Journal of Sport History* 4, no. 1 (1977): 72–83.
9. Florence Carpentier, "Alice Milliat: A Feminist Pioneer for Women's Sport," in *Global Sport Leaders: A Biographical Analysis of International Sport Management*, eds. Emmanuel Bayle and Patrick Clastres (London: Palgrave MacMillan, 2018), 61-81.
10. Ibid.
11. Gertrud Pfister, "Women and the Olympic Games," in *Women in Sport*, ed. Barbara Drinkwater (Oxford: Blackwell Science, 2000), 1-19.
12. Florence Carpentier and Jean-Pierre Lefèvre, "The Modern Olympic Movement, Women's Sport and the Social Order during the Inter-War Period," *The International Journal of the History of Sport* 23, no. 7 (2006): 1112-1127.
13. Carpentier and Lefèvre, "The Modern Olympic Movement."
14. Known as World Athletics since 2019.
15. Gutmann, *Women's Sports*, 167.
16. Krieger, Krech, and Pieper, "'Our Sport'."
17. Ibid.
18. Lindsay Parks Pieper, *Sex Testing: Gender Policing in Women's Sports* (Champaign: University of Illinois Press, 2016).

19. Cahn, *Coming on Strong*, 115.
20. Krieger, Krech, and Pieper, "'Our Sport'."
21. Susan E. Cayleff, *Babe: The Life and Legend of Babe Didrikson Zaharias* (Champaign: University of Illinois Press, 1996).
22. Ibid.
23. Pfister, "Women and the Olympic Games."
24. Ibid.
25. Jimoh Shehu, "African Women in Sports," in The Palgrave Handbook of African Women's Studies, ed. Olajumoke Yacob-Haliso and Toyin Falola (London: Palgrave MacMillan, 2019), 1-18.
26. Cindy Himes Gissendanner, "African American Women Olympians: The Impact of Race, Gender, and Class Ideologies, 1932-1968, Research Quarterly for Exercise and Sport 67, no. 2 (1996): 172-182.
27. Mary Louise Adams, "From Mixed-Sex Sport to Sport for Girls: The Feminization of Figure Skating," *Sport in History* 30, no. 2 (2010): 218-241.
28. Susan E. Cayleff, *Babe. The Life and Legend of Babe Didrikson Zaharias* (Champaign: University of Illinois Press, 1996).
29. Sharon Kinney-Hanson, *The Life of Helen Stephens: The Fulton Flash* (Carbondale: Southern Illinois University Press, 2004), 95-96.
30. Pieper, *Sex Testing*.
31. Ibid.
32. Gutmann, *Women's Sports*, 185.
33. Ibid., 182
34. James Riordan, "The Rise, Fall, and Rebirth of Sporting Women in Russia and the USSR," *Journal of Sport History* 18, no. 1 (1991): 183-199.
35. Sayuri Guthrie-Shimizu, "Diffusion and Transformation of Western Sports in North Asia," in *The Oxford Handbook of Sports History*, eds. Robert Edelman and Wayne Wilson (New York: University of Oxford Press, 2017), 276. Two men from Asia had participated individually at the 1900 Paris Olympic Games: Firidun Malkom Khan from Iran and Norman Gilbert Pritchard from India.
36. Alon K. Raab, "Sport in the Middle East," in *The Oxford Handbook of Sports History*, eds. Robert Edelman and Wayne Wilson (New York: University of Oxford Press, 2017), 292.
37. Claudia M. Guedes, "Empowering Women through Sport: Women's Basketball in Brazil and the Significant Role of Maria Helena Cardoso," *The International Journal of the History of Sport* 27, no. 7 (2010): 1237-1249.

Women in the Cold War Olympics

1. Robert Edelman and Christopher Young, *The Whole World Was Watching: Sport in the Cold War* (Stanford University Press, 2019), 1.
2. Alison Rowley, "Sport in the Service of the State: Images of Physical Culture and Soviet Women, 1941-1917," *The International Journal of the History of Sport* 23, no. 8 (2006): 1314-1340.
3. Gertrud Pfister, "A World Power in Women's Sport – Women Without Power in Sport: Gender, Power and Sport in East Germany," *Idrottsforum*, December 9, 2003, https://idrottsforum.org/articles/pfister/pfister.html/
4. Joseph M. Turrini, "'It Was Communism Versus the Free World': The USA-USSR Dual Track Meet Series and the Development of Track and Field in the United States,

1958-1985," *Journal of Sport History* 28, no. 3 (2001), 433.
5. Marina Kiblitskaya, "Russia's Female Breadwinners: The Changing Subjective Experience," in *Gender, State and Society in Soviet and Post-Soviet Russia,* ed. Sarah Ashwin (London: Routledge, 2000), 58.
6. Kateryna Kobchenko, "Emancipation within the Ruling Ideology: Soviet Women in Fizkul'tura and Sport in the 1920s and 1930s," in *Euphoria and Exhaustion: Modern Sport in Soviet Culture and Society,* eds. Nikolaus Katzer, Sandra Budy, Alexandra Köhring and Manfred Zeller (Frankfurt: Campus Verlag, 2010), 255-266.
7. Mike Dennis and Jonathan Grix, *Sport Under Communism: Behind the East German 'Miracle'* (Basingstoke: Palgrave MacMilan, 2012), 58.
8. Mihaela Andra Wood, *Superpower: Romanian Women's Gymnastics During the Cold War* (PhD diss., University of Illinois at Urbana-Champaign, 2010).
9. Amanda N. Schweinbenz, "Selling Femininity: The Introduction of Women's Rowing at the 1976 Olympic Games," *The International Journal of the History of Sport*, 26, no. 5 (2009), 660.
10. Dennis and Grix, *Sport Under Communism*, 49.
11. Ibid., 49.
12. Annabelle Quince and Keri Phillips, "A Question of Gender: The Sex Testing of Female Athletes," *Rear Vision* podcast, July 8, 2012, https://www.abc.net.au/radionational/programs/rearvision/a-question-of-gender-the-sex-testing-of-female/4087112.
13. Patricia Vertinsky, *Eternally Wounded Woman: Women, Doctors, and Exercise in Late Nineteenth Century* (University of Illinois Press, 1994).
14. Annemarie Jutel, "'Thou Dost Run as in Flotation': Femininity, Reassurance and the Emergence of the Women's Marathon," *The International Journal of the History of Sport* 20, no. 3 (2010): 17-36; Jaime Schultz, "Going the Distance: The Road to the 1984 Olympic Women's Marathon," *The International Journal of the History of Sport* 32, no. 1 (2015): 72-88.
15. Eleanor Metheny, "Symbolic Form of Movement: The Feminine Image in Sport," *Connotations of Movement in Sport and Dance: A Collection of Speeches about Sport and Dance as Significant Forms of Human Behavior* (Iowa: WM. C. Brown Company Publishers, 1964).
16. Schweinbenz, "Selling Femininity," 659.
17. Bruce Kidd, *The Struggle for Canadian Sport* (Toronto: University of Toronto Press, 2002), 121.
18. Robert L. Griswold, "'Russian Blonde in Space': Soviet Women in the American Imagination, 1950-1965," *Journal of Social History* 45, no. 4 (2012): 881.
19. Arthur Daley, "Sports of the Times: The Red-Faced Reds," *New York Times*, October 23, 1964, 47.
20. Sally Quinn, "The Sex Test," *Atlanta Constitution*, July 25, 1976, 8D.
21. Schweinbenz, "Selling Femininity," 660.
22. Cahn, *Coming on Strong,* 111-112.
23. Millie McDaniel finished first in the high jump; Willye White placed second in the long jump; and Isabelle Daniels, Wilma Rudolph, Mae Faggs Starr, and Margaret Matthews Wilburn earned bronze in the 4x100m relay.
24. Jennifer H. Lansbury, *A Spectacular Leap: Black Women Athletes in Twentieth-Century America* (Fayetteville: University of Arkansas Press, 2014).
25. Robert J. McMahon, *The Cold War on the Periphery: The United States, India, and Pakistan* (New York: Columbia University Press, 1996).
26. In official documentation, the date of the first participation of an Egyptian women is 1984. However, Amina Mahmoud participated in the qualification event at the 1972 Munich Olympics, comfortably qualifying for the final. Due to the Munich Massacre, the Egyptian delegation withdrew from the Games before the final was contested and

therefore Mahmoud could not compete in the medal event.

27. S.U. Anyanwu, "Issues in and Patterns of Women's Participation in Sports in Nigeria," *International Review for the Sociology of Sport* 15, no. 1 (1980): 85.
28. Ibid., 87.
29. Denise E.M. Jones, "Women and Sport in South Africa: Shaped by History and Shaping Sporting History," in *Sport and Women: Social Issues in International Perspective*, eds. Ilse Hartmann-Tews and Gertrud Pfister, 130-144 (Routledge: New York, 2003).
30. Lee Hill and Valérie Grand'Maison, "Swimming, South Africa and the Olympics: A History of Women's Participation," *Olympika* XXVI (2017), 41.
31. Participation numbers assessed from Olympedia.com.
32. East German athlete Birgit Radochla tied for second in the vault for the United Team of Germany.
33. Harald Lechenperg, ed., *Olympic Games 1964* (New York: A.S. Barnes and Co., 1964), 61.
34. Rob Beamish and Ian Ritchie, "Totalitarian Regimes and Cold War Sport: Steroid 'Ubermenschen' and "Ball-Bearing Females," in *East Plays West: Sport and the Cold War*, eds. Stephen Wagg and David L. Andrews (New York: Routledge, 2007), 22.
35. Letter to Johann Westerhoff from Donald T.P. Pain, December 14, 1967, IAAF Correspondence, 1967-1975, Archives of the International Olympic Committee, Olympic Studies Centre, Lausanne, Switzerland.
36. Mary Peters, *Mary P: Autobiography* (London: Stanley Paul & Company, Ltd., 1974), 56-57.
37. Murray L. Barr and Ewart G. Bertram, "A Morphological Distinction between Neurones of the Male and Female, and the Behaviour of the Nucleolar Satellite during Accelerated Nucleoprotein Synthesis," *Nature* 163, no. 4148 (April 30, 1949): 676-677
38. "Mosaic in X & Y," *Time*, September 29, 1967.
39. Minutes of the Meeting of the Medical Commission, July 14-17, 1968, Box 89, IOC Meetings, 1968, IOC Meetings—67th Session Folder, Avery Brundage Collection, University of Illinois Archives.
40. Beamish and Ritchie, "Totalitarian Regimes and Cold War Sport," 22.
41. Rob Beamish and Ian Ritchie, "The Spectre of Steroids: Nazi Propaganda, Cold War Anxiety and Patriarchal Paternalism," *The International Journal of the History of Sport* 5, no. 22 (2005): 777-795.
42. John Bale, "'Oscillating Antagonism': Soviet-British Athletic Relations, 1945-1960 in *East Plays West: Sport and the Cold War*, eds. Stephen Wagg and David L. Andrews (New York: Routledge, 2007), 82-99.
43. Thomas M. Hunt, *Drug Games: The International Olympic Committee and the Politics of Doping, 1960-2008* (Austin: University of Texas Press, 2011), 29.
44. Werner W. Franke and Brigitte Berendonk, "Hormonal Doping and Androgenization of Athletes: A Secret Program of the German Democratic Republic Government." *Clinical Chemistry* 43, no. 7 (July 1997), 1273.
45. Giselher Spitzer, "Sport and the Systematic Infliction of Pain: A Case Study of State-Sponsored Mandatory Doping in East Germany" in *The Ethics of Sport: A Reader,* ed. Mike McNamee (New York: Routledge, 2010), 413-425.
46. Neil Amdur, "Femininity or Prowess: U.S. Women must Choose," *Chicago Tribune,* August 2, 1976, E2.
47. Beamish and Ritchie, "Totalitarian Regimes and Cold War Sport," 21.
48. Schultz, *Qualifying Times: Points of Change in Women's Sport* (Urbana: University of Illinois Press, 214), 86.
49. Wayne Wilson, "The IOC and the Status of Women in the Olympic Movement: 1972-1996," *Research Quarterly for Exercise and Sport* 67, no. 2 (1996): 183-192.
50. Georgia Cervin, *Degrees of Difficulty: How Women's Gymnastics Rose to Prominence and Fell from Grace* (Champaign: University of Illinois Press, 2021).

Notes

51 Jim Murray, "Comaneci Olympics," *Los Angeles Times*, July 21, 1976, F1.
52 Extracts of the Minutes of the 65th Session of the International Olympic Committee, Tehran, May 6-8, 1967, *LA84 Foundation Digital Collections Library*, https://digital.la84.org/digital/collection/p17103coll1/id/28060/.
53 Florence Carpentier, Florys Castan-Vincente, and Claire Nicolas, "Women Sport Leaders During the Twentieth Century," *Digital Encyclopedia of European History*, https://ehne.fr/en/encyclopedia/themes/gender-and-europe/earning-a-living/women-sport-leaders-during-twentieth-century.
54 Laura F. Chase, "A Policy Analysis of Gender Inequality Within the Olympic Movement," *First International Symposium for Olympic Research*, February 1992, 30.

The Limited Liberation of Women in the Olympics by the End of the Century

1 "IOC Admits Its First Women," *The Tampa Times*, May 27, 1982, 11.
2 Estelle B. Freedman, *No Turning Back: The History of Feminism and the Future of Women* (New York: Random House Publishing Group, 2003), 5.
3 "Report of the Royal Commission on the Status of Women in Canada," 1970, https://women-gender-equality.canada.ca/en/commemorations-celebrations/royal-commission-status-women-canada.html, 406.
4 Mark Norman, Peter Donnelly, and Bruce Kidd, "Gender Inequality in Canadian Interuniveristy Sport: Participation Opportunities and Leadership Positions from 2010-11 to 2016-17." *The International Journal of Sport Policy and Politics* 13, no. 2 (2021): 207-223.
5 Parissa Safai, "Women in Sport Policy," in *Sport Policy and Canada*, eds. Lucie Thibault and Jean Harvey (Ottawa: University of Ottawa Press, 2013).
6 Sarah Fields, *Female Gladiators: Gender, Law, and Contact Sport in America* (Urbana: University of Illinois Press, 2008).
7 Jackie Joyner-Kersee, "Jackie Joyner-Kersee's Winning Moment," *ESPN*, June 5, 2012, https://www.espn.com/espnw/title-ix/story/_/id/8011246/jackie-joyner-kersee-winning-moment.
8 Vivian R. Acosta and Linda Jean Carpenter, "Women in Intercollegiate Sport: A Longitudinal, National Study. Thirty-Seven Year Update, 1977-2014. *ERIC*, 2014, https://eric.ed.gov/?id=ED570882.
9 Quoted in Pieper, Lindsay Parks. "Wolves in Skirts: Sex Testing in Cold War Women's Sports," in *Defending the American Wary of Life: Sport, Culture, and the Cold War*, eds. Toby C. Rider and Kevin B. Witherspoon (Fayetteville: Arkansas University Press), 91-92.
10 Cited in Jaime Schultz, "Going the Distance: The Road to the 1984 Olympic Women's Marathon," *The International Journal of the History of Sport* 32, no. 1 (2015): 76.
11 Ibid, 72.
12 Quoted in Cecile Houry, "American Women and the Modern Summer Olympic Games: A Story of Obstacles and Struggles for Participation and Equality," (PhD diss., University of Miami, 2011), 193.
13 Ibid., 193.
14 John W. Loy, Fiona McLachlan, and Douglas Booth, "Connotations of Female Movement and Meaning," *Olympika: The International Journal of Sport Studies* XVIII (2009): 1-24.
15 This table follows the US Department of Homeland Security's determination of global regions. The eight regions are Africa, Asia, Caribbean, Central America, Europe, North

America, Oceania, and South America.
16. Jordan J.K. Matthews, "Political Advances for Women and Sport in the Mid-1990s," *International Journal of Sport Policy and Politics* 13, no. 4 (2021), 641-659.
17. Brighton Declaration on Women in Sport, https://www.icsspe.org/sites/default/files/Brighton%20Declaration.pdf, 4.
18. Gertrud Pfister, "Women and Sport in Islamic Countries," *Idraet*, http://www.idan.dk/vidensbank/downloads/women-and-sports-in-islamic-countries/66143704-113b-41d5-aacc-a39500c1c799.
19. Maureen M. Smith and Alison Wrynn. *Women in the 2000, 2004, and 2008 Olympic and Paralympic Games: An Analysis of Participation, Leadership and Media Opportunities* (East Meadow: Women's Sport Foundation, 2009), https://search.issuelab.org/resource/women-in-the-2000-2004-and-2008-olympic-and-paralympic-games.html.
20. David Davis, "The Politics of Religion," *LA Weekly*, February 16, 1995, 162; Sara Eckel, "For Muslim Women, Olympics Mostly a Dream," *Capital Times*, July 89, 1996, 8A.
21. Gertrud Pfister, "Women and Sport in Iran: Keeping Goal in the *Hijab*," in *Sport and Women: Social Issues in International Perspective*, eds. Ilse Hartmann-Tews and Gertrud Pfister (London: Routledge), 207-223.
22. Geoff Harkness, "Out of Bounds: Cultural Barriers to Female Sports Participation in Qatar," *The International Journal of the History of Sport* 29, no. 15 (2012): 2162-2183.
23. Cagla Diner and Şule Toktaş, "Waves of Feminism in Turkey: Kemalist, Islamist and Kurdish Women's Movements in an Era of Globalization," *Journal of Balkan and Near Eastern Studies* 12, no. 1 (2010): 41-57.
24. Mahfoud Amara, "Veiled Women Athletes in the 2008 Beijing Olympics: Media Accounts," *The International Journal of the History of Sport* 29, no. 4 (2012): 638-651.
25. Tansin Benn and Symeon Dagkas, "The Olympic Movement and Islamic Culture: Conflict or Compromise for Muslim Women?" *International Journal of Sport Policy and Politics* 5, no. 2 (2013): 281-294.
26. "Muslim Women Seeking More Olympic Participation," *Scranton Times*, October 16, 1996, 19.
27. Moneque Walker Pickett, Marvin P. Dawkins, and Jomills Henry Braddock, "Race and Gender Equity in Sports: Have White and African American Females Benefitted Equally from Title IX?" *American Behavior Scientist* 56, no. 11 (2012): 1594.
28. D.W. Lawrence, "Sociodemographic Profile of an Olympic Team," *Public Health* (2017): 149-158.
29. Eric Schmitt, "Commercializing Olympic Champions," *New York Times*, April 28, 1985, https://www.nytimes.com/1985/04/28/business/commercializing-olympic-champions.html.
30. Margaret Carlisle Duncan, "Sports Photographs and Sexual Difference: Images of Women and Men in the 1984 and 1988Olympic Games," *Sociology of Sport* 7, no. 1 (1990): 22-43.
31. Quoted in Wayne Wilson, "The IOC and the Status of Women in the Olympic Movement: 1972-1996," *Research Quarterly for Exercise and Sport* 67, no. 2 (1996): 183-192.
32. Ibid.
33. International Olympic Committee, "Factsheet: Women in the Olympic Movement," *Olympics.com*, December 9, 2021, https://stillmed.olympics.com/media/Documents/Olympic-Movement/Factsheets/Women-in-the-Olympic-Movement.pdf.

Conclusion

1. Emily Houghton, Maureen M. Smith, and Lindsay Parks Pieper, *Women in the 2020 Olympic and Paralympic Games: An Analysis of Participation, Leadership, and Media Coverage* (East Meadow: Women's Sport Foundation, 2022); Emily Houghton, Maureen M. Smith, and Lindsay Parks Pieper, *Women in the 2022 Olympic and Paralympic Games: An Analysis of Participation, Leadership, and Media Coverage* (East Meadow: Women's Sport Foundation, 2023).
2. Houghton, Smith, and Pieper, *Women in the 2020 Olympic and Paralympic Games."*
3. Ibid.
4. International Olympic Committee Medical Commission, "Statement of the Stockholm Consensus on Sex Reassignment in Sports," 2003, http://multimedia.olympic.org/pdf/en_report_905.pdf
5. Sheila L. Cavanagh and Heather Sykes, "Transsexual Bodies at the Olympics: The International Olympic Committee's Policy on Transsexual Athletes at the 2004 Athens Summer Games," *Body and Society* 12, no. 3 (2006): 81.
6. Bill Littlefield, "Dutee Chand: A Woman Banned from Women's Sports," October 11, 2014, http://onlyagame.wbur.org/2014/10/11/dutee-chand-banned-iaaf; Patrick Fénichel et al., "Molecular Diagnosis of 5α-Reductase Deficiency in 4 Elite Young Female Athletes Through Hormonal Screening for Hyperandrogenismm," 1056.
7. Human Rights Watch, "They're Chasing Us Away from Sport," December 4, 2020, https://www.hrw.org/news/2020/12/04/end-abusive-sex-testing-women-athletes.
8. At the 2012 London Olympics, Semenya finished behind Russian runner Mariya Savinova. Savinova tested positive for a banned substance and was stripped of her gold medal.
9. "Semenya is South Africa's Golden Girl in 800," *Olympics.com*, https://olympics.com/en/news/semenya-is-south-africa-s-golden-girl-in-800m.
10. "Rio Olympics 2016," *New Zealand Herald*, August 23, 2016, https://www.nzherald.co.nz/sport/rio-olympics-2016-im-glad-im-the-first-european-olympian-shocks-with-racist-remarks/XBKZJAHTKN6INTDRZNYRHJFTFE/.

APPENDIX 1

Women's Olympic Participation, 1896-2022

Winter Olympics			Summer Olympics		
Olympics	No. of Women	No. of Men	Olympics	No. of Women	No. of Men
--	--	--	1896 Athens	0	241
--	--	--	1900 Paris	22	975
--	--	--	1904 St. Louis	6	645
--	--	--	1908 London	37	1,971
--	--	--	1912 Stockholm	47	2,359
--	--	--	1920 Antwerp	65	2,562
1924 Chamonix	11	247	1924 Paris	135	2,954
1928 St. Moritz	26	438	1928 Amsterdam	277	2,606
1932 Lake Placid	21	231	1932 Los Angeles	126	1,206
1936 Garmisch Partenkirchen	80	566	1936 Berlin	331	3,632
1948 St. Moritz	77	592	1948 London	390	3,714

Winter Olympics			Summer Olympics		
Olympics	No. of Women	No. of Men	Olympics	No. of Women	No. of Men
1952 Oslo	109	585	1952 Helsinki	519	4,436
1956 Cortina d'Ampezzo	134	687	1956 Melbourne	376	2,938
1960 Squaw Valley	144	521	1960 Rome	611	5,338
1964 Innsbruck	199	892	1964 Tokyo	678	5,151
1968 Grenoble	211	947	1968 Mexico City	781	5,516
1972 Sapporo	205	801	1972 Munich	1,059	6,075
1976 Innsbruck	231	892	1976 Montreal	1,260	4,824
1980 Lake Placid	232	840	1980 Moscow	1,115	4,064
1984 Sarajevo	274	998	1984 Los Angeles	1,566	5,263
1988 Calgary	301	1,122	1988 Seoul	2,194	6,197
1992 Albertville	488	1,313	1992 Barcelona	2,704	6,652
1994 Lillehammer	522	1,215	1996 Atlanta	3,523	6,797
1998 Nagano	787	1,389	2000 Sydney	4,069	6,582
2002 Salt Lake City	886	1,513	2004 Athens	4,329	6,296
2006 Turin	960	1,548	2008 Beijing	4,637	6,305
2010 Vancouver	1,043	1,536	2012 London	4,774	5,992
2014 Sochi	1,158	1,708	2016 Rio	5,059	6,000

Appendix 1 – Women's Olympic Participation, 1896–2022

Winter Olympics			Summer Olympics		
Olympics	No. of Women	No. of Men	Olympics	No. of Women	No. of Men
2018 Pyeongchang	1,204	1,704	2020/2021 Tokyo	5,486	5,998
2022 Beijing	1,276	1,581	--	--	--

Women's Disciplines/Sports Added, 1900-2022

APPENDIX 2

Olympics	Sport	Discipline
1900 Paris	Croquet	Individual
	Golf	Singles
	Tennis	Individual
1904 St. Louis	Archery	Individual
1908 London	Figure Skating	Singles
1912 Stockholm	Diving	10-meters platform
	Swimming	100-meters freestyle
		4x100-meters relay
1920 Antwerp	Diving	3-meters springboard
		10-meters platform
	Swimming	300-meters freestyle
	Tennis	Doubles
1924 Chamonix	Figure Skating	Singles
1924 Paris	Fencing	Foil individual
	Swimming	100-meters backstroke
		200-meters breaststroke
		400-meters freestyle
1928 St. Moritz	No additions	

Olympics	Sport	Discipline
1928 Amsterdam	Athletics	100-meters
		800-meters
		4x100-meters relay
		Discus throw
		High jump
	Gymnastics	Team all-around
1932 Lake Placid	No additions	
1932 Los Angeles	Athletics	80-meters hurdles
		Javelin
1936 Garmisch Partenkirchen	Alpine skiing	Combined
1936 Berlin	No additions	
1948 St. Moritz	Alpine skiing	Downhill
		Slalom
1948 London	Athletics	200-meters
		Long jump
		Shot put
	Canoeing	K-1 500-meters
	Gymnastics	Flying rings
1952 Oslo	Alpine skiing	Giant Slalom
	Cross-country skiing	10-kilometers
1952 Helsinki	Gymnastics	Balance beam
		Floor exercise
		Individual all-around
		Team portable apparatus
		Uneven bars
		Vault

Appendix 2 – Women's Disciplines/Sports Added, 1896-2022

Olympics	Sport	Discipline
1956 Cortina d'Ampezzo	Cross-country skiing	3x5-kilometers relay
1956 Melbourne	Swimming	100-meters butterfly
1960 Squaw Valley	Speed skating	500-meters
		1,000-meters
		1,500-meters
		3,000-meters
1960 Rome	Athletics	800-meters
	Canoeing	K-2 500-meters
	Fencing	Foil team
	Swimming	4x100-meters medley relay
1964 Innsbruck	Cross-country skiing	5-kilometers
	Luge	Singles
1964 Tokyo	Athletics	400-meters
		Pentathlon
	Swimming	400-meters individual medley
	Volleyball	Indoor
1968 Grenoble	No additions	
1968 Mexico City	Swimming	100-meters breaststroke
		200-meters backstroke
		200-meters butterfly
		200-meters freestyle
		200-meters individual medley
		800-meters freestyle
1972 Sapporo	No additions	

Olympics	Sport	Discipline
1972 Munich	Athletics	100-meters hurdles
		1,500-meters
		4x400-meters relay
	Canoeing	Slalom K-1
1976 Innsbruck	Figure skating	Ice dancing
1976 Montreal	Basketball	Team
	Handball	Team
	Rowing	Single sculls
		Double sculls
		Quadruple sculls
		Coxless pairs
		Eight
1980 Lake Placid	No additions	
1980 Moscow	Field hockey	Team
1984 Sarajevo	Cross-country skiing	20-kilometers
	Speed skating	5,000-meters
1984 Los Angeles	Artistic swimming	Solo
		Duet
	Athletics	400-meters hurdles
		3,000-meters
		Heptathlon
		Marathon
	Canoeing	K-4 500-meters
	Cycling	Road race
	Gymnastics	Rythmic

Appendix 2 – Women's Disciplines/Sports Added, 1896-2022

Olympics	Sport	Discipline
1984 Los Angeles	Shooting	Air rifle
		Pistol
		Rifle three positions
1988 Calgary	Alpine skiing	Super-G
1988 Seoul	Archery	Team
	Athletics	10,000-meters
	Cycling	Track sprint
	Sailing	470 fleet
	Shooting	Air pistol
	Swimming	50-meters freestyle
	Table tennis	Singles
		Doubles
1992 Albertville	Biathlon	7.5-kilometers sprint
		15-kilometers
		4x6-kilometers relay
	Cross-country skiing	15-kilometers
	Freestyle skiing	Moguls
1992 Barcelona	Athletics	10-kilometers walk
	Badminton	Singles
		Doubles
	Cycling	Track pursuit
	Judo	Extra lightweight
		Half lightweight
		Lightweight
		Half middleweight
		Middleweight

Olympics	Sport	Discipline
1992 Barcelona	Judo	Half heavyweight
		Heavyweight
	Rowing	Coxless four
	Sailing	Europe
		Lechner
1994 Lillehammer	Freestyle skiing	Aerials
1996 Atlanta	Artistic swimming	Team
	Athletics	5,000-meters
		Triple jump
	Cycling	Mountain biking
		Road time trial
		Track points race
		Track sprint
	Fencing	Individual epée
		Team épée
	Football (soccer)	Team
	Rowing	Lightweight double sculls
	Sailing	Mistral
	Softball	Team
	Swimming	4x200-meters freestyle relay
	Volleyball	Beach
1998 Nagano	Curling	Team
	Ice hockey	Team
	Snowboarding	Giant slalom
		Half-pipe

Appendix 2 – Women's Disciplines/Sports Added, 1896-2022

Olympics	Sport	Discipline
2000 Sydney	Athletics	20-kilometers walk
		Hammer throw
		Pole vault
	Cycling	Track time trial
	Diving	Synchronized 3-meters springboard
		Synchronized 10-meters springboard
	Gymnastics	Trampoline
	Modern pentathlon	Individual
	Shooting	Skeet
		Trap
	Taekwondo	Flyweight
		Lightweight
		Middleweight
		Heavyweight
	Triathlon	Individual
	Weightlifting	48 kilograms
		53 kilograms
		58 kilograms
		63 kilograms
		69 kilograms
		75 kilograms
		75+ kilograms
2002 Salt Lake City	Biathlon	10-kilometers pursuit
	Bobsleigh	Two-woman
	Skeleton	Individual

Olympics	Sport	Discipline
2002 Salt Lake City	Cross-country skiing	Individual sprint
	Snowboarding	Parallel giant slalom
2004 Athens	Athletics	10,000-meters
	Fencing	Individual sabre
	Sailing	Yngling
	Wrestling	Freestyle bantamweight
		Freestyle flyweight
		Freestyle heavyweight
		Freestyle middleweight
		Freestyle light heavyweight
		Freestyle welterweight
2006 Turin	Biathlon	12.5-kilometers mass start
	Cross-country skiing	Team pursuit
	Snowboarding	Snowboard cross
2008 Beijing	Athletics	3,000-meters steeplechase
	Cycling	Track 3,000-meters pursuit
		BMX racing
	Fencing	Team sabre
	Sailing	Laser radial
		RS:X
	Swimming	10-kilometers open water
2010 Vancouver	Freestyle skiing	Ski cross
2012 London	Boxing	Flyweight
		Lightweight
		Middleweight

Appendix 2 – Women's Disciplines/Sports Added, 1896-2022

Olympics	Sport	Discipline
2012 London	Canoeing	K-1 200-meters
	Cycling	Track keirin
		Track omnium
		Track team pursuit
		Track team sprint
	Sailing	Elliott 6m
2014 Sochi	Freestyle skiing	Half-pipe
		Slopestyle
	Ski jumping	Individual
	Snowboarding	Slopestyle
2016 Rio	Rugby	Sevens
2018 Pyeongchang	Snowboarding	Big air
	Speed skating	Mass start
2020/2021 Tokyo	Basketball	3x3
	Canoeing	C-1 200-meters
		C-2 500-meters
	Cycling	Track madison
	Karate	Individual
	Skateboarding	Park
		Street
	Sport climbing	Individual
	Surfing	Individual
	Swimming	1,500-meters
	Water polo	Team
2022 Beijing	Bobsleigh	Monobob
	Freestyle skiing	Big air

APPENDIX 3

Women's Debut by Country, 1900-2016

Information for Appendix 3 was derived from Olympedia.org. Current country names were used wherever possible. Countries that no longer exist are indicated by italics. First appearance of athletes refers to the first time an athlete from a country participated in an athletic event, though not necessarily as an official representative of the National Olympic Committee (NOC). In some instances, athletes competed prior to the organization and recognition of the NOC. Women's debut refers to the first time a woman from that country officially competed in an athletic event.

Country [First Appearance of Athletes]	Women's Debut	Number of Women	Number of Men
Bohemia [1900]	1900	1	6
France [1896]	1900	15	744
Great Britain [1896]	1900	1	95
Italy [1896]	1900	1	22
Switzerland [1896]	1900	2	16
United States [1896]	1900	4	66
Germany [1896]	1908	2	80
Sweden [1896]	1908	3	165
Australasia [1908]	1912	2	23

Country [First Appearance of Athletes]	Women's Debut	Number of Women	Number of Men
Austria [1896]	1912	6	79
Belgium [1900]	1912	1	34
Denmark [1896]	1912	1	151
Finland [1908]	1912	2	162
Norway [1900]	1912	2	188
Australia [1896]	1920	1	12
Czechoslovakia [1920]	1920	1	118
Netherlands [1900]	1920	1	129
New Zealand [1920]	1920	1	3
South Africa [1904]	1920	1	38
Canada [1904]	1924	1	11
Greece [1896]	1924	1	38
Hungary [1896]	1924	3	86
India [1920]	1924	1	12
Ireland [1924]	1924	2	46
Luxembourg [1912]	1924	2	46
Poland [1924]	1924	1	64
Spain [1900]	1924	2	93
Japan [1912]	1928	1	39
Latvia [1924]	1928	2	15
Lithuania [1924]	1928	1	11
Romania [1900]	1928	2	19
Brazil [1920]	1932	1	58
Guatemala [1932]	1932	1	20
Mexico [1924]	1932	2	71

Appendix 3 – Women's Debut by Country, 1900–2016

Country [First Appearance of Athletes]	Women's Debut	Number of Women	Number of Men
Argentina [1900]	1936	1	50
Chile [1912]	1936	1	39
China/People's Republic of China [1932]	1936	2	52
Estonia [1928]	1936	2	3
Turkey [1908]	1936	2	46
Yugoslavia (Montenegro, Serbia, Serbia and Montenegro) [1920]	1936	15	78
Bermuda [1936]	1948	2	10
Iceland [1908]	1948	3	18
Jamaica [1948]	1948	4	9
Republic of Korea [1948]	1948	1	45
Bulgaria [1924]	1952	9	54
Hong Kong, China [1952]	1952	2	2
Israel [1952]	1952	3	22
Portugal [1912]	1952	3	68
Saarland [1952]	1952	5	31
Singapore [1948]	1952	1	4
Soviet Union [1952]	1952	40	255
Uruguay [1924]	1952	1	31
Venezuela [1948]	1952	2	36
Cuba [1900]	1956	1	15
Guyana [1948]	1956	1	3
Indonesia [1952]	1956	2	20
Kenya [1956]	1956	1	24
Malaya [1956]	1956	1	32
Philippines [1924]	1956	4	35

Country [First Appearance of Athletes]	Women's Debut	Number of Women	Number of Men
Panama [1928]	1960	4	2
Puerto Rico [1948]	1960	1	26
Rhodesia [1960]	1960	5	7
Taiwan/Chinese Taipei/Formosa [1956]	1960	3	24
Democratic People's Republic of Korea [1964]	1964	7	6
Ghana [1952]	1964	3	30
Islamic Republic of Iran [1900]	1964	4	58
Malaysia [1964]	1964	4	57
Mongolia [1964]	1964	4	17
Nigeria [1952]	1964	2	16
Peru [1900]	1964	1	30
Thailand [1952]	1964	7	47
Uganda [1956]	1964	2	11
Zambia [1964]	1964	1	11
Zimbabwe [1928]	1964	4	25
Colombia [1932]	1968	5	38
Costa Rica [1936]	1968	1	17
Curaçao/Netherlands Antilles [1952]	1968	2	3
Ecuador [1924]	1968	1	14
El Salvador [1968]	1968	8	52
German Democratic Republic [1968]	1968	40	186
Liechtenstein [1936]	1968	1	8
South Vietnam [1952]	1968	2	7

Appendix 3 – Women's Debut by Country, 1900-2016

Country [First Appearance of Athletes]	Women's Debut	Number of Women	Number of Men
Albania	1972	1	4
the Bahamas [1952]	1972	1	19
Barbados [1968]	1972	5	8
Cambodia [1956]	1972	1	8
Haiti [1900]	1972	1	6
Lebanon [1948]	1972	2	17
Malawi [1972]	1972	3	13
Morocco [1960]	1972	2	33
Nicaragua [1968]	1972	1	7
Syrian Arab Republic [1948]	1972	1	4
Trinidad and Tobago [1948]	1972	1	18
Ivory Coast (Côte d'Ivoire) [1964]	1976	1	7
Dominican Republic [1964]	1976	1	9
Fiji [1956]	1976	1	1
San Marino [1960]	1976	2	8
Senegal [1964]	1976	2	19
Tunisia [1960]	1976	1	14
United States Virgin Islands [1968]	1976	2	19
Angola [1980]	1980	1	10
Benin [1972]	1980	1	15
Cameroon [1964]	1980	3	22
Congo [1964]	1980	14	9
Cyprus [1980]	1980	2	12
Ethiopia [1956]	1980	2	39
Lao People's Democratic Republic [1980]	1980	2	17

Country [First Appearance of Athletes]	Women's Debut	Number of Women	Number of Men
Libya [1968]	1980	2	27
Madagascar [1964]	1980	3	8
Mali [1964]	1980	1	6
Malta [1928]	1980	1	7
Mozambique [1980]	1980	2	12
Seychelles [1980]	1980	2	9
Sierra Leone [1968]	1980	2	12
United Republic of Tanzania [1964]	1980	5	36
Vietnam [1980]	1980	8	22
Antigua and Barbuda [1976]	1984	4	10
Bhutan [1984]	1984	3	3
Bolivia [1936]	1984	1	10
Cayman Islands [1976]	1984	1	7
Democratic Republic of the Congo [1968]	1984	1	7
Egypt [1920]	1984	6	108
Gabon [1972]	1984	2	2
The Gambia [1984]	1984	4	6
Grenada [1984]	1984	1	5
Honduras [1968]	1984	3	7
Jordan [1980]	1984	1	12
Liberia [1956]	1984	1	6
Mauritius [1984]	1984	1	3
Papua New Guinea [1976]	1984	3	4
Rwanda [1984]	1984	1	2

Appendix 3 – Women's Debut by Country, 1900-2016

Country [First Appearance of Athletes]	Women's Debut	Number of Women	Number of Men
Algeria [1964]	1988	2	40
Andorra [1976]	1988	2	2
Aruba [1988]	1988	4	4
Burkina Faso [1988]	1988	5	1
Cook Islands [1988]	1988	1	6
Equatorial Guinea [1984]	1988	2	4
Guam [1988]	1988	5	14
Monaco [1920]	1988	1	8
Myanmar [1948]	1988	2	0
Nepal [1964]	1988	3	13
Saint Vincent and the Grenadines [1988]	1988	1	5
Sri Lanka [1972]	1988	2	4
Suriname [1968]	1988	2	4
Tonga [1984]	1988	1	4
Vanuatu [1988]	1988	1	3
Bangladesh [1984]	1992	1	5
Belize [1968]	1992	1	9
Bosnia Herzegovina [1992]	1992	4	6
Central African Republic [1968]	1992	2	13
Chad [1964]	1992	1	5
Croatia [1992]	1992	36	3
Guinea [1968]	1992	2	6
Lesotho [1972]	1992	1	5
Maldives [1988]	1992	1	6
Namibia [1992]	1992	1	5

Country [First Appearance of Athletes]	Women's Debut	Number of Women	Number of Men
Paraguay [1968]	1992	3	24
Slovenia [1992]	1992	6	29
Belarus [1994]	1994	12	21
Czech Republic [1994]	1994	16	47
Kazakhstan [1994]	1994	10	19
Kyrgyzstan [1994]	1994	1	0
Republic of Moldova [1994]	1994	1	1
Russian Federation [1994]	1994	75	38
Slovakia [1994]	1994	8	34
Ukraine [1995]	1994	17	20
Uzbekistan [1994]	1994	4	3
American Samoa [1988]	1996	1	6
Armenia [1994]	1996	2	30
Azerbaijan [1996]	1996	3	20
Burundi [1996]	1996	1	6
Cape Verde [1996]	1996	1	2
Comoros [1996]	1996	1	3
Dominica [1996]	1996	2	4
Eswatini [1972]	1996	1	5
Georgia [1994]	1996	7	27
Niger [1964]	1996	1	2
North Macedonia [1996]	1996	3	8
Pakistan [1948]	1996	1	23
Saint Kitts and Nevis [1996]	1996	6	4
Saint Lucia [1996]	1996	1	5

Appendix 3 – Women's Debut by Country, 1900-2016

Country [First Appearance of Athletes]	Women's Debut	Number of Women	Number of Men
São Tomé and Príncipe [1996]	1996	1	1
Samoa [1984]	1996	1	4
Solomon Islands [1984]	1996	1	3
Tajikistan [1996]	1996	2	6
Turkmenistan [1996]	1996	3	4
Bahrain [1984]	2000	2	2
Djibouti [1984]	2000	1	1
Eritrea [2000]	2000	1	2
Federated States of Micronesia [2000]	2000	2	3
Guinea Bissau [1996]	2000	1	2
Iraq [1948]	2000	2	2
Mauritania [1984]	2000	1	1
Nauru [1996]	2000	1	1
Palau [2000]	2000	3	2
Palestine [1996]	2000	1	2
Somalia [1972]	2000	1	1
Sudan [1960]	2000	1	2
Togo [1972]	2000	1	2
Yemen [1992]	2000	1	1
Afghanistan [1936]	2004	2	3
Botswana [1980]	2004	1	10
Kiribati [2004]	2004	1	2
Kuwait [1968]	2004	1	10
Timor Leste [2004]	2004	1	1

Country [First Appearance of Athletes]	Women's Debut	Number of Women	Number of Men
British Virgin Islands [1984]	2008	1	1
Marshall Islands [2008]	2008	2	3
Montenegro [2008]	2008	2	17
Oman [1984]	2008	1	3
Serbia [2008]	2008	24	63
Tuvalu [2008]	2008	1	2
United Arab Emirates [1984]	2008	2	6
Brunei Darussalam [1996]	2012	1	2
Kingdom of Saudi Arabia [1972]	2012	2	16
Qatar [1984]	2012	4	8
Kosovo [2016]	2016	5	3
South Sudan [2016]	2016	1	2

www.ingramcontent.com/pod-product-compliance
Lightning Source LLC
Chambersburg PA
CBHW032158160426
43197CB00008B/965